The Toyota
Management System

The Toyota Management System

Linking the Seven Key Functional Areas

Yasuhiro Monden

Translated by
Bruce Talbot

Most Productivity Press books are available at quantity discounts when purchased in bulk. For more information contact our Customer Service Department (888-319-5852). Address all other inquires to:

Productivity Press
444 Park Avenue South, Suite 604
New York, NY 10016
United States of America
Telephone 212-686-5900
Fax: 212-686-5411
E-mail: info@productivitypress.com

Book and cover design by Gary Ragaglia
Printed and bound by: Edwards Brothers Incorporated
Printed in the United States of America on acid-free paper

Library of Congress Cataloging-in-Publication Data

Monden, Yasuhiro. 1940-
    The Toyota management system: linking the seven key functional areas/Yasuhiro Monden; publisher's message by Norman Bodek; translated by Bruce Talbot.
        p. cm.
    Translated from the Japanese.
    Includes bibliographical references and index.
    ISBN 1-56327-139-7
    1. Automobile factories — Management.   2. Just-in-time systems.
3. Toyota Jidosha Kabushiki Kaisha.
TL278.M66   1993
629.23'4 — dc20   92-27133
                                                            CIP

Contents

Tables and Figures

Original Publisher's Message

FOR OVER A DECADE, manufacturers have gazed wide-eyed while Toyota Motors has risen to astonishing heights. In the West, we study Toyota's production system with its just-in-time (JIT) and kanban methodologies and try to adapt it to our own workplaces. In truth, amony my reasons for founding Productivity Press was so that I could purchase English-language rights to the Japanese work of manufacturing giants such as Taiichi Ohno and Shigeo Shingo. These two early Toyota men were responsible for the development and ultimate success of this world-class manufacturer.

We all realize, of course, that Toyota's success is based on more than any single production technique. These days, in fact, it is difficult to think of Toyota in strictly manufacturing terms because it has gone so far beyond. Consider the breadth of its marketing and sales management, consider its new product development, financial management, international production strategy, and so on. Fortunately, Yasuhiro Monden does it for us in this fine book., *The Toyota Management System: Linking the Seven Key Functional Areas.*

Recognized worldwide for his knowledge of the Japanese automobile industry, Dr. Monden was instrumental in the early 1980s in bringing information about the JIT production system to the United States. He has written numerous books for Western readers, including the 1984 classic *Toyota Production System* and *Japanese Management Accounting: A World Class Approach to Profit Management*, which Productivity published in 1989. Currently professor of managerial accounting and production management at the University of Tsujuba, he has been a visiting professor at California State University in Los Angeles and at the State University of New York in Buffalo. He also serves on the editorial board of the American Accounting Association's Journal of Management Accounting Research. As these credentials show, Dr. Monden is a respected authority on both sides of the Pacific.

While much has been written about various aspects of Toyota's production system, this is the first book to examine the unified, all-encompassing management system to successfully evolve in the process. Eight chapters describe Toyota's financial management system; profit management; its companywide cross-functional management; its "flat" organizational system and personnel management; its dales management system; new product development; production management (and how it incorporated a strategic information system [SIS], computer-integrated manufacturing [CIM], and just-in-time methods); and, lastly, its international production strategy.

There is something here for people in all areas of a company — and for all kinds of companies. The wisdom that has evolved from Toyota's manufacturing environment is broader than one industry. It can serve many. Taiichi Ohno recognized this and talked about it in his book *Just-In-Time for Today and Tomorrow*. And now, we see just that. We find JIT ideas applied to restaurants (Kentucky Fried Chicken), convenience stores (7-Eleven), public utilities (Florida Power & Light), chemicals (Exxon), computers (Iomega), and communications (AT&T). The list goes on — but it would be better for you to read this book and consider how to apply it for yourself.

Nearly a decade ago I resolved to publish in English informative and sometimes provocative books by Japan's thinkers and doers in management and manufacturing. Japan's financial and industrial evolvement in the post-World War II and now post-Cold War era has made this of great importance to us globally and nationally. And I, among others, feel that we have much to learn about our Pacific neighbors.

As always, it takes many people to create a book and I wish to acknowledge them: Bruce Talbot, translator; Cheryl Rosen, acquisitions and project editor; Bill Berling, freelance copyeditor; Dorothy Lohmann, managing editor; Laura St. Clair, assistant editor; Jennifer Cross, indexer; David Lennon, production manager; Karla Tolbert, typesetter; and Gary Ragaglia, cover designer. I have known the author since 1980 when he addressed an American audience about the new Japanese manufacturing mentality. I have followed his progress since and speak for all us at Productivity in saying that we are honored to publish another of his fine books.

Norman Bodek

Preface

WHAT IS THE BEST way to
develop, produce, and market goods and services? And how
should a company raise the capital needed for investing in
such an undertaking? How should costs be planned and
managed to make sure the end result is "profitability?" What
is an effective way to develop production and sales activities
on a global scale? And how can the company develop an
organization that enables employees to respond flexibly to
their fast-changing environment?

Today, companies in many industries face management
issues such as these. This book attempts to explain how companies can practice effective management as they undertake
these basic management activities. I have decided to use the
Toyota Motor Company as the sole source for the case studies
contained in this book in order to describe more systematically
one of the world's most effective management systems.

Many books have been written about Toyota's production
management system, also known as the "Just-In-Time
Production Method" (JIT). However, this is the first to present
a comprehensive and systematic description of Toyota's

entire management system, which includes not only production management but also research and development (R&D) management, sales management, financial management, cost planning, organizational management, and the planning of international production strategy.

The reader might question the need for a book describing Toyota's entire management system. I feel the necessity because Toyota's production management system is actually a subsystem that does not exist separately from the company's overall management system. The functions of these subsystems are mutually supportive functions, so that the production management subsystem exchanges support with the sales subsystem, new product development subsystem, financial management subsystem, personnel subsystem, and so on. This mutual support among subsystems is a key factor contributing to the excellent performance of Toyota's overall management system.

One point I have tried to emphasize in this book is the interdependence between *management functions* and *manufacturing functions*. To carry out its more socially significant function of making products, Toyota has integrated a wide range of management functions into its production system to make the production functions more effective in serving the needs of society. (This will also be addressed in the Introduction.)

This book's target readership includes — and goes beyond — the ranks of top managers who oversee large corporate organizations that encompass many skill categories. It is also intended for middle managers in each type of corporate division and skill category as a reference for improving their management activities. I am especially hopeful that this book will be read by production department managers because I feel they have much to gain by better understanding how peripheral departments relate to their own departments.

Finally, this book should be useful to students and employees aspiring toward management careers as a textbook on the latest advances in Japanese management methods and a systematic study of Japanese corporate management.

I will conclude by offering my heartfelt thanks to Mr. Kazuya Uchiyama of the Japan Management Association, who again has lent invaluable and extensive support in the publication of my work.

Introduction

A Unified System of Business Management: The Pursuit of Effectiveness

SINCE World War II, Japanese companies have pursued "effectiveness" as a chief management principle. Effectiveness means being able to respond to environmental changes and also to achieve the company's objectives in an efficient, waste-free manner. The strong competitiveness of Japanese companies in the global marketplace springs from the highly effective management systems these companies have developed. With its broad scope, the Toyota management system described in this book is a typical example.

Toyota Motor Corporation is involved in a wide range of activities and makes various kinds of contributions to society, the principal contribution being its role as a manufacturer of automobiles. In this book, we shall look into what functions Toyota carries out as an automaker, how it has woven various management skills into the fabric of its production system, and how Toyota's production functions effectively contribute to society.

To make "things," manufacturing company managers must first gather together and make effective use of human and financial resources; in other words, people and money. Accordingly, this study describes how managers prepare for production by procuring funds and how they manage those funds. We call this the financial management system.

Since the main objective in investing money is to make a profit, one of the manufacturer's functions is to minimize production costs to leave room for profits. We will examine the cost planning methods Toyota uses.

We will also see why companies need a personnel organization that both enables and encourages people to put energy and enthusiasm into their work.

After that, we will examine the strengths of Toyota's sales organization — its automobile sales network. Sales is a primary motivating force for manufacturing since there is no point in manufacturing anything unless the sales outlets are able to sell it. We will also look at Toyota's steps for new product development, its narrowly defined production steps, and its strategy for international production.

Following are brief summaries of each chapter's contents and how they tie in with manufacturing functions.

CHAPTER 1: FINANCIAL MANAGEMENT SYSTEM

The function of financial management is to achieve a balance between capital procurement and capital application. Manufacturing companies should not procure capital purely for the sake of security portfolio investment. At Toyota, each new car model requires a minimum investment of $365 million (¥ 50 billion) in new car development work and corresponding new equipment. How does Toyota come up with that kind of money? We will find out as we examine Toyota's capital procurement and application system for financing new products. In so doing, we will also study Toyota's approach toward managing security portfolio investment.

CHAPTER 2: TARGET COSTING AND KAIZEN COSTING IN THE JAPANESE AUTOMOBILE INDUSTRY

As a profit-oriented company, Toyota strives to realize a yearly net profit and seeks to return dividends to its shareholders. To ensure profitability, Toyota must supply funds for plant investment and other purposes. In order to achieve its long-term and annual profit targets, Toyota plans ways to keep costs down in a *target costing* system initiated at the new product development stage. Later, at the production stage, Toyota carries out a series of further cost-saving improvements in a *kaizen costing* system.

CHAPTER 3: FUNCTIONAL MANAGEMENT

While U.S. automakers have decentralized organizations composed of many profit center divisions, Toyota's organization is fully centralized. Therefore, the responsibility for establishing communication links between the various departments at Toyota and ensuring cooperation and coordination in implementing companywide quality control and cost management is given to an organizational unit called a *functional meeting*.

This is a top management decision unit that makes policy decisions and action plans for implementing in each department.

CHAPTER 4: FLAT ORGANIZATIONAL AND PERSONNEL MANAGEMENT

Toyota has introduced what it calls a "flat organization" in which the *just-in-time* approach has been applied to decision making among middle and lower managers throughout the company to prevent decision-making delays. We will examine the structure and operation of this flat organization.

CHAPTER 5: SALES MANAGEMENT SYSTEM

Sales is the function that enables the production function to operate. Smooth daily production of goods is only possible when certain large numbers of those goods can be sold. The number of goods sold is determined largely by the appeal of the goods themselves and by *sales strength*, which is a product of factors such as the number of sales outlets and the abilities of the sales and promotion people. This chapter will look at Toyota's sales strength and the special features of the Toyota sales network.

CHAPTER 6: NEW PRODUCT DEVELOPMENT SYSTEM

For automakers, the new product development system is the starting point in the process of creating new cars. This process begins with market surveys and new product planning and continues with exterior and interior design, body and main parts design, prototype fabrication and testing, line setup, and so on. For certain car models, Toyota designates a single person as the car's chief engineer; this person is responsible for the entire development process. This chapter examines how Toyota cars are designed and developed under this *chief engineer system*.

CHAPTER 7: PRODUCTION MANAGEMENT SYSTEM: SIS, CIM, AND JIT

How does the end user's order information flow between the car sales agent on the one hand and Toyota and its parts suppliers on the other? This chapter describes Toyota's *Strategic Information System (SIS)* that provides a network enabling such sales information to flow more efficiently. How does Toyota apply today's advanced data processing and electronic communications technologies to keep tabs on the equipment, people, and goods at its various assembly plants? The answer is Toyota's *Computer-integrated Manufacturing (CIM)* system that allows each factory to operate autonomously as it does under the famous *kanban* system. Finally, we examine the *just-in-time (JIT)* aspects of Toyota's Production Management System. This helps ensure that only products that can be sold reach the market, and that they reach the market only in the required amounts and at the required delivery time.

CHAPTER 8: INTERNATIONAL PRODUCTION STRATEGY

This chapter looks at the globalization strategies of Toyota and other Japanese automakers, including their international strategies for parts procurement.

On the whole, this book is intended to enlighten readers as to how Toyota links its activities with its primary social role as a manufacturer and how it achieves its primary goal of raising production effectiveness in its myriad forms, such as flexibility, quick responsiveness, productivity, and profitability.

CHAPTER ONE

Financial Management System

WHEN WE REFER to a company's financial management system we mean the decision-making process related to the procurement and application of capital. This chapter examines Toyota's financial management system.

Japan's business environment has undergone great changes, both during the oil crises of the 1970s and during the yen's steep climb against the dollar that began in the mid-1980s. These environmental changes have forced Japanese companies to become more dependent on capital from outside investors and more heavily burdened by interest obligations.

It sometimes happens that capital resources run dry, creating a life-or-death situation for the company. To avoid such predicaments, companies must build for themselves a financial structure that can withstand the kind of dramatic environmental changes that have occurred in recent years.

When the business environment is a favorable one, it is relatively easy for companies to procure both internal and external capital. The main purposes for such capital include funds for new plant investment, new product development, or for working capital. Any funds left over after serving these purposes usually are channeled toward safe and profitable investments in vehicles that lie outside the company's main fields of business.

During an economic recession or depression, companies must move to protect their main business activities. At such times they are also wise to put the funds accumulated through their effective management of capital assets during the economic boom years into short-term, high-yield investments that provide safe alternatives to main business investments. In fact, companies always need such external investments as a source of capital that can be readily channeled toward new business opportunities.

The point of the strategy just described is to stop looking outside the company for capital procurement and to instead use funds produced by the company itself. When the need for funds is large, however, these internal fund-raising methods may not be enough, and the company may decide to turn to fund-raising methods such as issuing convertible corporate bonds or warrant bonds (certificates with preemptive rights), methods which are likely to change the nature of the company's own capital assets. We refer to this type of financing as "equity financing," or capital procurement through new stock issues.

While acknowledging that the type of financial operations described previously varies somewhat from company to company and industry to industry, we can say with certainty that all companies work with the same basic rules, policies, and know-how in managing their financial operations.

This chapter analyzes the financial data of Toyota Motor Corporation, known today for its debt-free management and for its top ranking as a company that stays "in the black."

These data cover the years 1974 to 1988. We will look at how Toyota has procured and managed its capital assets to support its automobile production and sales organizations. Specifically, we will study the rules, policies, and know-how behind Toyota's financial management system and will identify the basic principles of its corporate financial operations.

SPECIAL FEATURES OF TOYOTA'S CAPITAL PROCUREMENT METHODS

What are the special features of the capital procurement methods used by Toyota? Table 1-1 shows Toyota's capital procurement trends over several years. As shown, Toyota clearly is oriented toward in-house capital procurement, for which it maintains vast amounts of retained profit and large depreciation expenses.

The retained profit reserves are what are left of the company's net (after tax) profits for each business term after the company allots dividends (including interim dividends) to shareholders and pays executive bonuses. From business year 1974 (BY74) to BY85, such retained income generally expanded. However, in BY78, BY79, and BY81, such funds shrank slightly from the previous year's level. The drop in BY78 was caused chiefly by the stricter controls on new-car exhaust emissions, the BY79 drop by the second oil crisis, and the BY81 drop by the Japanese auto industry's adoption of voluntary export restrictions on passenger cars sold in the United States and Canada. The slight reductions that occurred from BY86 to BY88 came under the impact of the yen's rapid appreciation against the U.S. dollar.

Depreciation expenses are the costs related to paying off the costs of depreciated items. As such, depreciation expenses are used to turn fixed assets into current assets or to recover invested capital. This makes depreciation expenses one of the

Table 1-1. Capital Procurement Trends (1974-1988)

(unit: ¥1 million)

	(External Capital)		Year	(Internal Capital)		Total: Cash Flow
Capital Increase	Increase in Corporate Bonds	Short-term Loans Outstanding	Year	Internal Retained Profit	Depreciation Expenses	Total: Cash Flow
28	0	0	49 (1974)	31,401	63,308	94,709
0	0	3,770	50 (1975)	61,323	127,468	188,791
22,834	0	569	51 (1976)	89,535	69,231	158,766
37,474	0	0	52 (1977)	101,802	61,231	163,033
44	0	0	53 (1978)	98,856	74,832	173,688
1	0	0	54 (1979)	83,328	90,054	173,382
32,554	0	0	55 (1980)	120,456	105,632	226,098
0	0	0	56 (1981)	107,767	121,005	228,772
99,051	0	0	57 (1982)	114,368	156,887	271,255
10,188	0	63,410	58 (1983)	164,682	173,456	338,138
0	0	0	59 (1984)	211,211	163,360	380,571
6,046	0	0	60 (1985)	260,865	174,373	435,238
6,347	0	0	61 (1986)	205,394	194,907	400,301
0	200,000	0	62 (1987)	150,421	220,259	370,680
2,480	117,760	0	63 (1988)	188,164	224,419	412,583

resources for in-house capital procurement. Although depreciation expenses declined slightly from previous-year levels in BY76, BY77, and BY84, on the whole they grew during the period of BY74 to BY88. The declines in BY76 and BY77 were caused by Toyota's curtailment of new plant investment in order to recover capital during the production slowdown that came in the wake of the first oil crisis.

We refer to the sum of a company's internal retained profits and depreciation expenses as the company's "internal capital." Analysts keep a close watch on the size of a company's internal capital as the company deals with changes in the economic environment.

At Toyota, there has been relatively little capital procurement from outside sources (that is, external capital). In fact, Toyota showed absolutely no external capital in its business results for BY81 and BY82, which underscores just how little the company relies on outside sources of capital.

Looking at more specific categories, we see that Toyota showed annual increases in short-term loans in BY75, BY76, and BY83. The BY83 jump, however, was caused by the merger of Toyota Motor Company with Toyota Motor Sales Company, an upturn that was reversed in the next year. Therefore, in real terms Toyota has operated under "debt-free management" (without a "loans" account title) since BY77.

Although Toyota's corporate bonds increased in BY87 and BY88, the corporate bonds issued in BY87 were U.S. dollar-based convertible bonds that were used primarily for meeting the funding needs of overseas projects such as the construction of assembly plants and other facilities in the United States. (As of 1992, one U.S. dollar equaled ¥ 130.) In BY88, ¥ 2.48 billion of these funds were converted to internal capital. Also in BY88, Toyota issued U.S. dollar-denominated warrant bonds which were also used for plant investments in the United States. Because Toyota's results for BY88 were based on a business year that ended on June 30, 1988, neither the BY88 balance sheet nor the schedule of bonds payable showed Toyota's major bond issue of ¥ 30 billion in convertible bonds that took place on July 28, 1988, based on board decisions made on June 20 and July 11, 1988. Toyota issued these bonds to make use of the high yen and the voluntary car export curbs and as a manifestation of its U.S.-based projects that now covered activities ranging from capital procurement to automobile production and sales as operation of that capital.

Toyota shows a certain amount of fluctuation in its capital increases from year to year. Later in this chapter we will examine how capital operations (or meeting capital demand) relate to such increases. For the time being, please note which years have served as the main years for procuring new capital (such as BY77, during which Toyota raised ¥ 99 billion).

From what we have just observed, we can point to debt-free management and reliance on internal capital (especially retained profits) as the two primary special features of capital procurement at Toyota. These features did not change much even after 1986, when the yen's sharp rise against the U.S. dollar began making its full impact felt. This is because convertible bonds, unlike other liabilities, are converted easily into internal capital. Also the issuing of warrant bonds is a capital procurement method that facilitates the augmentation of internal capital.

Another special feature of financial management at Toyota is the way the company sells off short-term bonds and sets short bond maturity periods of less than a year as a well-timed method to procure short-term funds. To analyze this method, we must approach it from both the capital procurement and capital application perspectives, and we will do so later in the chapter.

SPECIAL FEATURES OF CAPITAL APPLICATIONS (RESPONSES TO CAPITAL NEEDS) AT TOYOTA

Previously, when we identified the two primary special features of capital procurement at Toyota, we noted the very strong emphasis Toyota puts on retained profits as an internal capital source. Table 1-2 shows the degrees to which operating profits from Toyota's main business and its finance-based revenues (non-operating profits minus non-operating expenses) based on financial activities have contributed to its net income before taxes.

In studying Table 1-2, please note the following definitions:

1. Share of operating profits = operating profits ÷ net income before taxes
2. Share of finance-based revenues = (non-operating profits − non-operating expenses) ÷ net income before taxes

While the main business (operating profit) continues over the years to dominate Toyota's net income before taxes, we still see a general rise in the share of finance-based (non-operating) revenues. This trend testifies to Toyota's relative stability in turning out successful results in its main business even when dealing with a changing economic environment. That is why we see much larger shares of finance-based revenues during years when total income before taxes are relatively low. In this manner, Toyota has responded to short-term depressions affecting its main business activities by strengthening the support provided by its financial activities. From this, we come to understand how Toyota has managed to be so strongly resistant to recessions in the automobile industry.

In other words, Toyota's strength in automobile manufacturing operations is backed up firmly by its skill in security portfolio investment.

Table 1-2. Shares of Operating Profits and Finance-based Revenues

(Unit: Percentage share × ¥1 million)

Business Year	Net Income before Taxes (Value)	Operating Profit		Finance-based Revenues	
		Value	Share (%)	Value	Share (%)
49 (1974)	45,608	22,903	50.2	15,857	34.8
50 (1975)	125,455	83,079	66.2	25,953	20.7
51 (1976)	192,659	148,561	77.1	37,509	19.5
52 (1977)	217,877	167,678	77.0	44,163	20.3
53 (1978)	206,786	153,082	74.0	45,721	22.1
54 (1979)	200,658	158,289	78.9	40,045	20.0
55 (1980)	288,668	233,232	80.8	58,348	20.2
56 (1981)	227,511	140,183	61.6	87,327	38.4
57 (1982)	298,489	230,513	77.2	75,670	25.4
58 (1983)	402,872	304,543	75.6	94,048	23.3
59 (1984)	516,767	406,482	78.7	115,285	22.3
60 (1985)	648,009	505,891	78.1	142,118	21.9
61 (1986)	488,385	329,387	67.4	158,998	32.6
62 (1987)	398,008	248,364	62.4	149,644	37.6
63 (1988)	521,706	369,087	70.7	152,619	29.3

Let us now look at the special features of Toyota's capital operations. Table 1-3 lists various detailed data concerning Toyota's capital operations. These data were compiled from annual securities reports for the period of BY82 to BY88, and all values are based on ledger balances, or book values, established immediately after June 30 — the end of each business year.

Table 1-3 lists Toyota's capital applications in the following three categories. We will examine their special features in greater detail.

1. applications in tangible fixed assets
2. applications in security portfolio investment outside of the main business
3. applications in support of affiliated *(keiretsu)* companies

APPLICATIONS IN TANGIBLE FIXED ASSETS

These are Toyota's investments in its main business. Most of these funds are used for plant investment. Between BY81 and BY87, the total funds in this category increased steadily until BY88, when tangible fixed assets dropped nearly ¥ 19 billion from their BY87 level. However, it probably will not be long before tangible fixed assets rise to reach the ¥ 1 trillion mark.

This type of main-business investment is needed to maintain a high level of production capacity and to help earn operating profits. As such, it is essential for the ongoing improvement of management and the development of the business. For automakers such as Toyota, main-business investment — especially plant investment for developing new car models — is the major investment theme for the company's financial managers.

APPLICATIONS IN SECURITY PORTFOLIO INVESTMENT OUTSIDE OF THE MAIN BUSINESS

Most of these funds are channeled into four types of investment vehicles:

Table 1-3. Detailed Data Concerning Toyota's Capital Applications

(Unit: ¥1 million)

Business Year (ending June 30)	56 (1981)	57 (1982)	58 (1983)	59 (1984)	60 (1985)	61 (1986)	62 (1987)	63 (1988)
(Tangible Fixed Assets)	582,352	615,954	735,682	722,293	768,293	929,393	982,119	962,966
(Working Assets)								
Cash Deposits	103,102	118,031	171,811	607,132	588,161	574,898	845,993	1,083,128
Securities	122,717	362,967	598,431	318,403	461,756	303,450	212,886	133,338
Investment Securities	196,207	184,628	213,352	260,216	281,478	295,348	334,035	365,840
Investment Stock in Affiliated Companies	148,370	162,191	163,481	186,251	203,416	221,588	258,710	344,685
Investment Bonds in Affiliated Companies	0	0	1,500	500	3,896	4,236	22,238	41,018
Contributions to Affiliated Companies	780	615	880	862	852	852	852	864
Long-term Loans Receivable from Affiliated Companies	6,897	5,978	20,184	23,912	23,246	25,045	31,689	13,738
Long-term Loans Receivable from Employees	42,167	47,708	62,778	67,715	65,761	60,938	51,816	12,083
Long-term Loans Receivable	8,482	6,905	26,819	23,785	19,446	18,360	18,150	21,960
Long-term Time Deposits	20,000	20,000	27,500	38,099	221,992	267,335	295,124	431,177

(Unit: ¥1 million)

(Breakdown of Cash Deposits)

Current, Ordinary, and Call Time	19,699	9,100	⎫ 497,132	462,661	⎫ 514,748	829,993	1,493
Time Deposits	83,332	156,211	⎭		⎭		1,046,905
Negotiable Time Deposits	15,000	6,500	110,000	125,000	60,150	16,000	0
Cash in Trust	0	0	0	0	0	0	34,730

(Breakdown of Securities)

Stocks	0	5	3	0	4	2	6
Public Bonds, Government Bonds, and Regional Bonds	362,967	598,426	318,399	461,756	303,446	212,883	133,331

(Breakdown of Investment Securities)

Stocks (for Affiliated Structure)	104,009	129,144	133,421	136,793	140,256	152,118	162,225
Public Bonds, Government Bonds, and Regional Bonds	75,375	76,530	120,229	136,295	145,130	173,810	193,177
Other	5,244	7,677	6,565	8,390	9,962	8,106	10,436

- cash and bank deposits
- securities (almost all are bonds rather than stocks)
- bonds as long-term investment securities
- long-term time deposits

CAPITAL APPLICATIONS IN CASH AND DEPOSITS The total amount of Toyota's cash and deposits took a major jump in BY84. In the wake of this big surge there were slight annual reductions in BY85 and BY86. However, cash deposits increased again in BY87, reaching nearly ¥ 85 billion; in BY88 they passed the ¥ 1 trillion mark. This put cash/deposits at a higher level than tangible assets for the BY63 term. Why did Toyota channel so much money toward cash deposits instead of main-business investments? We can see why by examining Table 1-3's cash/deposit breakdown. The four types of cash/deposits listed are: (1) checking, ordinary, and call deposits; (2) time deposits; (3) negotiable deposits; and (4) cash in trust. Note that in its annual securities reports for BY84 to BY87, Toyota lumped together the first two types.

If we compare time deposits for the years BY82 and BY88, we see that total time deposits were multiplied by a factor of 12.56 over this period. In BY88, they constituted almost 97 percent of the total cash deposits that exceeded ¥ 1 trillion. Undoubtedly, Toyota recognized the large-sum, variable-interest time deposits, first introduced in October 1985, as an attractive investment vehicle. Indeed, the further liberalization of Japan's finance and capital markets created many profitable new opportunities for time deposit investors. This explains why Toyota invested so much in time deposits over the years from BY84 to BY87.

Negotiable deposits offer the following five advantages: (1) they are freely negotiable, (2) they are variable-interest deposits with high investment yields, (3) they are sold in units of ¥ 50 million or above, (4) their time periods range from over two weeks to under two years, and (5) they are legally classified as deposits and exempt from Japan's securities transaction tax. Toyota made extensive use of this investment vehicle from the time it was introduced in May 1979. It soon owned such a large share of negotiable deposits that analysts began referring specifically to Toyota's share of the negotiable deposit market as the "Toyota rate." However, due to the later introduction of large-sum, variable-interest time deposits, Toyota's negotiable-deposit investments peaked in 1985 and then subsided rapidly before hitting zero in 1988. One reason for Toyota's abandonment of negotiable deposits was that they failed to earn interest after reaching maturity.

Toyota began to use the "cash in trust" investment method in 1988. This method, in which companies entrust cash to trust and banking companies who in turn invest it in stocks, bonds, and other vehicles, has gained popularity only recently in Japan. Since Toyota is known as a company that insists on safe high-yield investments, Toyota's financial experts no doubt have chosen only those trust and banking companies that specify exactly which kinds of vehicles they use for its entrusted funds. (Some trust and banking companies do not specify this.)

CAPITAL APPLICATIONS IN SECURITIES These are all short-term securities holdings, nearly all of which are bonds — either public bonds, government bonds, or regional bonds. Toyota has invested only ¥ 2 million to ¥ 6 million in stocks — relatively little indeed — and that has been largely in temporary acquisition of Toyota's own stock as required by fractional trading. These data reflect Toyota's securities policy of investing only in safe, high-yield bonds.

One method that has become popular among companies that are looking for short-term uses for ordinary surplus capital is the bonds with future resale value. Toyota has taken full advantage of what these investment vehicles have to offer. Bonds with future resale value are bought on the condition that they will be sold after a specified period of time. Their value can be determined freely, which makes them a variable-yield investment. The time periods for such bonds must not exceed one year, and actual transactions have been based on time periods ranging from a minimum seven days to a maximum of about six months, with a typical range of one to three months. The interest rate is set through negotiations with the relevant securities firms and banks prior to concluding the sale contract. Once the contract is signed, the terms are totally unaffected by stock market trends.

These conditions make temporary bonds a safe and reliable high-yield vehicle for very short-term investments that help the investor retain a high degree of liquidity. Naturally, temporary bonds have had to compete with other short-term investment vehicles. Since they are subject to the securities transaction tax, their yield has been slightly less than some other investment vehicles, such as negotiable deposits, that offer similar interest rates but are not subject to the securities transaction tax. These and other competing vehicles, such as large-sum, variable-interest time deposits, gradually lured Toyota away from temporary bonds. The result is that Toyota has invested only minimally in temporary bonds since 1985.

CAPITAL APPLICATIONS IN BONDS AS LONG-TERM INVESTMENT SECURITIES These are not temporary bonds but rather ordinary long-term bonds. Interest is paid to the bond holder each term until the redemption date when the principal is returned to the investor. This is what makes such bonds a convenient investment vehicle. Toyota's bonds in this category steadily increased between 1982 and 1988.

CAPITAL APPLICATIONS IN LONG-TERM TIME DEPOSITS This has been a fast-growing area of investment for Toyota since 1985, as Toyota has increasingly opted for large-sum, variable-interest time deposits. With time periods of one year or more, these time deposits have more restrictions than other investments that fall under the "cash deposits" category. However, banks sorely need time deposit investors as a key source of deposits. One would suppose that this supply-and-demand situation gives Toyota a strong hand when negotiating interest rates on such time deposits with banks. By 1988, Toyota's total investment in these time deposits exceeded ¥ 430 billion.

(unit: ¥1 million)

Year		Total Capital
57	(1982)	272,793
58	(1983)	315,189
59	(1984)	344,946
60	(1985)	368,203
61	(1986)	391,977
62	(1987)	465,607
63	(1988)	562,530

Table 1-4. Total Capital Invested in Affiliated Companies

SPECIAL FEATURES OF APPLICATIONS IN SUPPORT OF AFFILIATED COMPANIES

The production and sale of automobiles entails a long series of processes. New model development occurs in unison with body and parts manufacturers because the major automakers depend so much on these supplier companies. They also depend heavily upon dealers when it comes to selling their products. Car sales generally involve finance companies as well. Most of these companies belong to Toyota's affiliate organization *(keiretsu)* and enjoy stable, long-term relationships with Toyota. Such affiliate relationships are vital to all Japanese automakers. As a result, Toyota's automobile business is operated by a group that includes Toyota and its affiliated companies.

Large amounts of capital operations must be devoted toward maintaining this organization. Refer to the five subcategories of capital applications that fall under this category in Table 1-3. These are:

1. stocks within long-term investment securities
2. investment stock in affiliated companies
3. investment bonds in affiliated companies
4. contributions to affiliated companies
5. long-term loans receivable from affiliated companies

Table 1-4 shows total funds that Toyota invested in support of its affiliated companies from 1982 to 1988. We can see a steady increase in these investments each year.

Looking at Table 1-3, we can see that Toyota's stock investments in affiliated companies (under the categories investment stock in affiliated companies and stock within investment securities) increased without exception year after year.

Almost all of Toyota's consolidated subsidiaries are dealer companies and 60 to 70 percent of its nonconsolidated subsidiaries are involved in the transportation industry. Toyota Motor Credit, a U.S.-based finance company, is a nonconsolidated subsidiary under the equity method. Japan-based Nippondenso, an auto parts manufacturing and sales company, is a nonsubsidiary affiliate in which Toyota Motor nevertheless owns a large equity share.

It is noteworthy that, during this period, the companies in which Toyota owned stock as investment securities included banks such as the Tokai Bank, Mitsui Bank, and Sanwa Bank, as well as various other companies across a wide range of industries.

As for the third subcategory, investment bonds in affiliated companies, Toyota first made these types of investments in BY83, then eased off from them the following year. It decided to increase them somewhat in BY85 and BY86 and then channeled more funds into them in BY87 and BY88. All such investments were in corporate bonds issued by affiliated companies.

The fourth subcategory, contributions to affiliated companies, includes both subsidiary and nonsubsidiary affiliates. The total here increased from ¥ 615 million to about ¥ 880 million.

As for the fifth subcategory, long-term loans receivable from affiliated companies, the total showed a sharp increase in BY83, stayed about even from BY85 to BY86, then rose again in BY87 before rapidly declining in BY88 as Toyota shifted funds toward other types of investments.

To summarize the special features of Toyota's capital operations: Toyota has been very active in capital operations involving tangible, fixed assets, which is only natural since these funds are devoted to Toyota's main business. However, Toyota has also been careful to establish strong resistance to recessions in the automotive industry by channeling surplus capital into safe, variable-interest investments outside of its main business.

With regard to capital operations outside of its main business, Toyota has responded expertly to changes in Japan's finance and capital markets and to the easing of restrictions and the appearance of new types of investment vehicles. Toyota has consistently concentrated such capital in investment vehicles that are conducive to highly effective capital operations.

Concerning its investments in affiliated companies, Toyota has recognized how essential it is that the entire Toyota group of companies be supported to help improve the flow of processes that includes delivery of materials and parts, production, distribution, sales, collection of fees, after-sales service, and so on, as well as the flow of related finance activities. This has required an increasing amount of investment from Toyota. When we examine the energetic way in which Toyota has invested in its affiliated companies, we can see that Toyota's management policy has been one of strengthening ties within the Toyota group and furthering the group's development.

THE RELATIONSHIP BETWEEN CAPITAL PROCUREMENT AND CAPITAL APPLICATIONS

The main theme of financial management in any company is the pursuit of corporate growth and profitability while maintaining financial stability in terms of balancing the company's capital procurement and capital operations. Tables 1-5 and 1-6 present capital demand data that describe how this balance between capital procurement and capital operations has been maintained over the years. (Table 1-5 presents Toyota business years 1974 (BY74) to BY81; Table 1-6 presents BY82 to BY88.)

The following is a year-by-year summary of the relationship between capital procurement and capital applications at Toyota.

- *BY74.* Still struggling to recover from the 1973 oil crisis, Toyota posted a low net profit and was unable to increase its tangible fixed assets due to a lack of retained profits. In addition, Toyota was forced to sell off some of its securities holdings to raise capital for meeting its obligations for corporate bonds, long-term debts, and other long-term accounts payable.
- *BY75.* Although it achieved a higher net profit this year, Toyota had to meet investment obligations that had been passed on from the previous year as well as its corporate bonds and long-term loans. The result was another year of capital shortages.
- *BY76.* Investment in tangible fixed assets dwindled to a mere 30 percent of the previous year's level as more surplus capital was channeled toward supporting affiliated companies. Toyota raised more capital for bond redemption and increased outlays to parts suppliers. A major improvement in total sales created expectations for greater sales volume. By way of preparation for this future volume growth, Toyota boosted its inventory assets investment 260 percent, and also achieved a shorter turnover period than in the previous business year. The net profit took a solid step upward. All in all, Toyota achieved a good balance in internal capital procurement and operations in BY76.
- *BY77.* Total sales increased 14.65 percent, a rate similar to the previous year's sales improvement. Much of the increased capital was channeled toward investment in tangible fixed assets, which grew 245 percent over the previous year. Meanwhile, investment in support of affiliated companies shrank to 60 percent of the previous year's level. Some funds also went toward bond

Table 1-5. Capital Supply and Demand Statistics (BY74 to BY81)

Business Year	49 (1974)	50 (1975)	51 (1976)	52 (1977)	53 (1978)	54 (1979)	55 (1980)	56 (1981)
Net Profit	39,147	73,841	99,559	116,777	116,286	102,058	143,568	132,727
Dividend Allotments (Subtracted)	7,616	12,294	9,844	14,755	17,180	18,480	22,802	24,640
Executive Bonuses (Subtracted)	130	224	180	220	250	250	300	320
Retained Profits	31,401	61,323	89,535	101,802	98,856	83,328	120,466	107,767
Depreciation Expenses (Added)	63,308	127,468	69,231	61,231	74,832	90,054	105,632	121,005
Cash Flow	94,709	188,791	158,766	163,033	173,688	173,382	226,098	228,772
Increase in Tangible Fixed Assets (Subtracted)	129,007	149,679	44,273	108,560	144,924	117,360	136,151	274,125
Capital Surpluses or Deficits	34,298	39,112	114,493	54,473	28,764	56,022	89,947	45,353
Reduction in Securities (Added)	54,186	208	0	0	9,880	0	0	150,064
Increase in Securities (Subtracted)	0	0	3,345	5,362	0	9,860	91,354	0
Balance Total	19,888	39,320	111,148	49,111	38,644	46,162	1,407	104,711
Increase in Investments and Other Assets (Subtracted)	4,448	7,454	43,903	26,032	8,878	37,233	87,709	56,874
Balance	15,440	31,866	67,245	23,079	29,766	8,929	89,116	47,837
Increase in Capital (Added)	28	0	22,834	37,474	44	1	32,554	0
Increase in Corporate Bonds (Added)	0	0	0	0	0	0	0	0
Increase in Long-term Accounts Payable (Added)	0	0	0	0	0	0	5,010	0
Other (Added)	0	0	0	0	0	0	0	0
Total	15,468	31,866	90,079	60,553	29,810	8,930	51,552	47,837
Reduction in Corporate Bonds (Subtracted)	2,256	3,636	4,300	4,152	4,152	0	0	0

Reduction in Long-term Loans (Subtracted)	601	272	0	0	0	0	0	0
Reduction in Long-term Accounts Payable (Subtracted)	284	0	79	0	4,941	401	0	4,973
Balance	12,327	27,958	85,700	56,401	20,717	8,529	51,552	42,864
Provision for Accrued Retirement Allowances (Added)	8,903	32,078	5,776	4,926	13,671	8,003	8,302	9,279
Appraised Loss due to Liquidation of Assets (Added)	0	1,375	1,558	1,940	0	3,183	4,625	4,389
Other (Added)	0	0	895	3,342	0	440	2,543	1,186
Total	21,230	61,411	93,929	66,609	34,388	20,155	36,082	57,718
Recovered Reserves (Subtracted)	2,988	33,448	9,421	8,457	9,283	10,324	7,088	3,715
Other (Subtracted)	0	22,130	894	690	59	0	3,463	2,924
Balance	18,242	5,833	83,614	57,462	25,046	9,831	46,633	51,079
Increase in Sales Credit (Subtracted)	1,056	80,815	54,390	40,003	60,427	49,383	47,064	41,317
Increase in Inventory Assets (Subtracted)	4,631	32,821	87,226	43,519	129	2,126	19,382	2,736
Increase in Other Fluid Assets (Subtracted)	2,148	2,442	74	1,821	958	483	192	144
Balance	10,407	110,245	58,076	27,881	36,210	42,161	113,271	12,354
Increase in Reserve for Bad Debts (Added)	0	4,305	1,247	1,030	858	0	906	1,129
Increase in Trade Payables (Added)	2,914	49,716	19,660	14,561	37,945	11,345	32,281	21,316
Increase in Short-term Loans (Added)	0	3,770	569	187	0	0	0	0
Increase in Other Short-term Liabilities (Added)	23,899	52,491	36,511	11,945	1,871	40,698	88,784	36,199
Increase in Cash Deposits	16,406	37	89	532	4,464	9,882	8,700	3,658

Table 1-6. Capital Supply and Demand Statistics (BY82 to BY88)

(Unit: ¥1 million)

Business Year	57 (1982)	58 (1983)	59 (1984)	60 (1985)	61 (1986)	62 (1987)	63 (1988)
Net Profit	141,589	201,372	251,567	308,309	255,185	200,208	238,006
Dividend Allotments (Subtracted)	26,901	36,270	39,897	46,972	49,319	49,319	49,334
Executive Bonuses (Subtracted)	320	420	459	472	472	468	508
Retained Profits	114,368	164,682	211,211	260,865	205,394	150,421	188,164
Depreciation Expenses (Added)	156,887	172,456	169,360	174,373	194,907	220,259	224,419
Cash Flow	271,255	338,138	380,571	435,238	400,301	370,680	412,583
Increase in Tangible Fixed Assets (Subtracted)	198,977	304,813	144,158	214,613	361,028	278,459	210,142
Capital Surpluses or Deficits	72,278	33,325	236,413	220,625	39,273	92,221	202,441
Reduction in Securities (Added)	0	0	280,031	0	158,306	90,564	79,548
Increase in Securities (Subtracted)	240,251	235,464	0	143,356	0	0	0
Balance Total	167,973	202,139	516,444	77,269	197,579	182,785	281,989
Increase in Investments and Other Assets (Subtracted)	5,065	87,616	84,890	219,159	73,637	121,940	218,829
Balance	173,038	289,755	431,554	141,890	123,942	60,845	63,160
Increase in Capital (Added)	99,051	10,188	0	6,046	6,347	0	2,480
Increase in Corporate Bonds (Added)	0	0	0	0	0	200,000	117,760
Increase in Long-term Accounts Payable (Added)	0	0	0	0	0	0	0
Other (Added)	0	268,999	0	0	0	0	0
Total	173,987	10,568	431,554	135,844	130,289	260,845	183,400
Reduction in Corporate Bonds (Subtracted)	0	0	0	0	0	0	2,480

Reduction in Long-term Loans (Subtracted)	0	0	0	0	0	0	0
Reduction in Long-term Accounts Payable (Subtracted)	0	228	0	0	0	0	0
Balance	73,987	10,796	431,554	135,844	130,289	260,845	180,920
Provision for Accrued Retirement Allowances (Added)	10,528	24,879	13,354	16,128	15,038	16,680	16,211
Appraised Loss Due to Liquidation of Assets (Added)	9,533	12,288	0	12,156	11,956	9,558	6,950
Other (Added)	1,770	0	18,049	3,701	0	2,661	53
Total	52,156	26,371	462,957	103,859	157,283	289,744	204,134
Recovered Reserves (Subtracted)	2,307	7,987	26,723	0	0	0	0
Other (Subtracted)	1,045	659	0	17,390	8,270	4,084	2,074
Balance	55,508	17,725	436,234	121,249	149,013	285,660	202,060
Increase in Sales Credit (Subtracted)	16,796	69,961	49,716	45,078	24,251	22,335	94,028
Increase in Inventory Assets (Subtracted)	7,554	90,096	15,964	3,293	30,264	18,356	8,444
Increase in Other Fluid Assets (Subtracted)	3,912	159,603	2,370	5,040	23,601	30,363	44,606
Balance	88,770	162,013	368,184	174,660	131,425	214,606	54,982
Increase in Reserve for Bad Debts (Added)	1,666	12,628	330	231	4,485	2,033	3,848
Increase in Trade Payables (Added)	8,836	69,613	27,758	21,643	15,683	4,830	39,863
Increase in Short-term Loans (Added)	0	63,410	63,410	0	0	0	0
Increase in Other Short-term Liabilities (Added)	88,197	70,142	102,459	134,277	155,886	63,352	138,442
Increase in Cash Deposits	14,929	53,780	435,321	18,971	13,263	271,095	237,135

redemption. BY77 was another well-balanced year for internal capital procurement and operations.

- *BY78.* Net profits were off slightly, but internal capital continued to expand. Investment in tangible fixed assets grew 133 percent over BY87. A little capital was siphoned off from securities investments and funneled into affiliated companies. Other capital went toward bond redemption and long-term accounts payable. Toyota achieved a major shortening of the turnover period for inventory assets. These and other results led to a cash deposit increase of ¥ 4,464 million.
- *BY79.* Both sales growth and net profits were down in the wake of the second oil crisis. Toyota responded by maintaining its main business at current levels. Accordingly, surplus capital was channeled toward investments in support of affiliated companies and buying more securities. As a result, cash deposits rose 220 percent over BY78.
- *BY80.* Toyota worked hard to improve its main business. It managed to recover from the second oil crisis and post an annual improvement in net profits. Sales jumped 18.12 percent over BY79. Some internal capital went toward increased investment in tangible fixed assets, but the bulk was channeled into investments outside the main business (particularly securities buying, which jumped roughly 927 percent) and toward affiliated companies. This created a capital shortage which Toyota met by raising more than ¥ 32.5 billion.
- *BY81.* Despite a slowing of sales growth, Toyota worked energetically to increase investment in tangible fixed assets. This led to an annual reduction in net profits. Because internal capital was not sufficient to cover this higher investment in tangible fixed assets,

Toyota sold off some of its extensive securities holdings to fill the gap. Toyota also disbursed funds into long-term accounts payable.

- *BY82*. This year, internal capital more than sufficed to cover investment in tangible fixed assets. However, Toyota also went on a securities buying spree and had to procure capital to cover these costs.
- *BY83*. The total sales figure soared as Toyota Motor merged with Toyota Motor Sales. However, this was not enough to meet all of Toyota's capital needs. The accounting results for BY83 are a complicated array of counterbalancing increases and reductions as a result of the big merger, and it is very difficult to analyze their overall significance. All short-term debts shown for this year were inherited from Toyota Motor Sales.
- *BY84*. Investment in tangible fixed assets were down from the previous year's level, which produced surplus internal capital that was funneled into paying off short-term loans and boosting investment in support of affiliated companies. Funds freed through securities liquidations were shifted toward negotiable deposits and time deposits. Net profits were up from the previous year.
- *BY85*. Net profits jumped 9.2 percent higher than the previous year's level. Internal capital left over after covering investments in tangible fixed assets were sent, along with some procured capital, into buying more securities and investing in support of affiliated companies.
- *BY86*. Tangible, fixed assets grew at their highest level in fifteen years. Internal capital, along with liquidated securities and procured capital, was channeled toward tangible, fixed assets and affiliated companies.

Cash deposits shrank due to a major disposition of reserves for short-term liabilities.

- *BY87.* Net profits plummeted under the impact of the yen's steep climb against the dollar. If we assume that almost all funds devoted to increased investment in fixed tangible assets went toward covering Toyota's U.S. dollar-denominated convertible bond issues, then the funds procured through securities sales were used for higher investments in support of affiliated companies and large-sum, variable-interest time deposits.

- *BY88.* Toyota began recovering from the high yen's impact. Net profits were up. All funds from the new corporate bond issues were used, along with some of Toyota's internal capital, to fill capital needs for increased tangible fixed assets investment, then the rest of the internal capital and the capital procured from securities liquidation went into outside investments such as large-sum, variable-interest time deposits, cash in trust, and support for affiliated companies.

CONCLUSION

Let us now summarize this chapter's presentation of the facts regarding Toyota's capital procurement and applications.

1. To a very large extent, Toyota has tended to procure capital through so-called internal capital which consists largely of retained profits and depreciation expenses. Even when Toyota turns to external sources to procure capital, such procurement is usually covered by owner's capital (stock) increases and convertible bonds. Consequently, we can recognize how Toyota has remained firmly committed to meeting its own capital needs in line with its policy of debt-free management.

2. To maintain and expand its capital from retained profits, Toyota has emphasized its positive support for plant investment, new car development funding, and investment in support of affiliated companies. Nevertheless, Toyota has also recognized the need for an external security net for its main business, which is very sensitive to economic downturns. Therefore, it also has pursued capital operations outside the main business that can be counted upon to remain profitable regardless of conditions affecting the automotive industry. Such operations have concentrated on investing in negotiable deposits; temporary bonds; large-sum, variable-interest time deposits; and other investment vehicles that offer safe, reliable, and high-yield returns. Toyota has been conspicuous for its strong aversion to stock-market investments. This conservative approach is seen as part of Toyota's staunch policy of putting its main business before all other considerations.

3. When increased investment toward tangible, fixed assets cannot be covered by Toyota's internal capital, Toyota has tended to liquidate some of its massive securities holdings.

4. Whenever Toyota has found itself with excess capital, it has tended to channel such capital toward further investments in support of affiliated companies or for acquiring more securities.

5. Whenever Toyota's main business has floundered amid depressed business conditions, Toyota has eased off on its tangible fixed assets investment and shifted more funds into outside investments and support for affiliated companies.

Finally, one point worth noting with regard to the relationship between Toyota's financial management system and its production management system is that the latter's success in drastically reducing inventory levels for materials, parts, in-process goods, and products has minimized the need to tie up funds in such inventory assets. This has contributed greatly to the company's financial management.

CHAPTER TWO

Target Costing and Kaizen Costing in the Japanese Automobile Industry*

ENVIRONMENTAL changes in the Japanese automobile industry are severe — for example, the high appreciation of the yen, the shortening of the product life cycle, the diversification of demand, and keen competition. Cost management methods must be useful for (1) the production of new products that meet customers' demands at lowest cost as well as for (2) the cost reduction of existing products by eliminating waste.

Therefore, companies today require a total cost management system that includes product development and design activities as well as production activities. This contrasts with traditional cost management, which focused on cost control in the production stage. The fact that most costs in the production stage are determined in the stage of new product development and design indicates the need for total cost management.

---

* This material, co-written by Professor Kazuki Hamada of Seinan Gakuin University, was first published in the Fall 1991 issue of *Journal of Management Accounting Research*. It is reprinted with permission.

This chapter describes the features of the total cost management system in Japanese automakers. Its two main pillars are *target costing* (establishing and attaining a target cost) and *kaizen costing*. They can be summarized as follows:

- *Target costing* (or *genkakikaku*) is the system to support the cost reduction process in the development and design phase of an entirely new model, a full model change, or a minor model change.
- *Kaizen costing* (or *genkakaizen*) is the system to support the cost reduction process in the manufacturing phase of the existing product model. The Japanese word *kaizen* differs slightly from the English word "improvement." Kaizen refers to the continuous accumulations of small improvement activities rather than innovative improvement. Therefore, kaizen costing includes cost reduction in the manufacturing stage of existing products. Innovative improvement based on new technological innovations usually is introduced in the development and design stage.[1]

Target costing and kaizen costing, when linked together, constitute the total cost management system of Japanese companies. "Total" cost management in this context implies cost management in all phases of product life. The concept of total cost management also comes from total involvement of all people in all departments companywide.

Since the concept of kaizen costing is rather new in the United States, we will clarify its concept, procedures, and relationships with target costing. The general idea seems to be that floor-level control activities are more useful in modern manufacturing plants as a result of the spread of the just-in-time (JIT) production system and total quality control (TQC), and that the accounting control system has become useless.

We would like to demonstrate, however, that the management accounting system functions well in both target costing and kaizen costing in Japanese automakers.

FEATURES OF TARGET COSTING

In broad terms, the step of corporate long- or middle-term profit planning is included in the process of target costing. A more narrow interpretation would have target costing consist of two processes roughly classified as: (1) the process of planning a specific product that satisfies customers' needs and of establishing the target cost from the target profit and targeted sales price of the new product, and (2) the process of realizing the target cost by using value engineering (VE) and a comparison of target costs with achieved costs.[2]

The basic idea of VE is that products and services have functions to perform and the amount of their value is measured by the ratio of these functions to their costs. By this process, the decision as to whether the product is to be produced is made. For this purpose, it is necessary that the functions of each product, part, and service are clarified and that all functions are quantified. For example, VE activities for direct materials can be implemented concerning the material quality or a grade change, the reduction of the number of bolts in a part, the change of a part shape, the common use of an alternative part, the change of painting method, and so on.

VE differs from control activities based on traditional standard cost accounting and it encourages the proposal of creative plans designed to reduce cost standards. This contrasts with standard cost accounting, which overemphasizes the determination and achievement of cost performance standards.

The VE techniques were first developed at General Electric by Lawrence D. Miles. In GE's case, however, they initially aimed at reducing the costs of purchased parts. Hence, their VE activities were not linked to corporate target profit and target costs as they are in Japan.

Target costing has the following general properties:

1. It is applied in the development and design stage and differs from the standard cost control system applied in the production stage.
2. Although it intends to reduce costs, it is not a management method for cost control in a traditional sense.
3. In the target costing process, many management science methods are used because managerial goals include the techniques of development and product design.
4. The cooperation of many departments is needed in its execution.
5. Target costing is more suitable in wide variety, small-lot production than in the mass production of a few products.

Other reasons why target costing has become important is that in Japan the ratio of variable costs to total manufacturing costs has increased remarkably in recent years (up to 90 percent in the auto industry); the ratio of direct material costs to total variable costs is about 85 percent. This means that the management of variable costs is increasingly important. Moreover, as the ratio of direct labor costs to total manufacturing costs is about 6 percent among automakers, managing direct material costs by target costing has become more important than managing direct labor costs.

Though the direct object of consideration in target costing is costs, target costing must be closely connected with corporate profit planning. Take for example, the case of a company that can develop products whose sales prices greatly exceed their high costs because of their high quality. If a company focuses only on costs, there may be a bias against high cost/high profit products. By linking target costing and profit planning, such a bias can be prevented. It also allows employees to understand that a company's ultimate goal is not cost reduction but higher profits.[3]

For our purposes we will divide the target costing process into the following five steps: corporate planning, developing the specific new product project, determining the basic plan for a specific new product, product design, and the production transfer plan.[4] Figure 2-1 outlines the target costing system.

THE TARGET COSTING SYSTEM

STEP 1: CORPORATE PLANNING

In Step 1, the long-and medium-term profit plans for the entire company are established and the overall target profit for each period is determined for each product. In the three-year profit plan, marginal income (sales price − variable costs), contribution margin (marginal income − traceable fixed costs), and operating profit (contribution margin − allocated fixed costs) as average figures for a series of developing models are computed. Based on this average figure, each of these three kinds of profits is planned for several representative types of each model. In computing operating profits, depreciation costs of facilities and dies, development costs, and prototype manufacturing costs are allocated to each model. Often the return-on-sales ratio is used to indicate the profit ratio for establishing target profit, because this ratio is computed easily for each product.

A corporate plan is drafted by the corporate planning department. As part of the process, new product development plans are drafted by the engineering planning department and a general new product plan is established. In this plan, the time frame of new product development, model

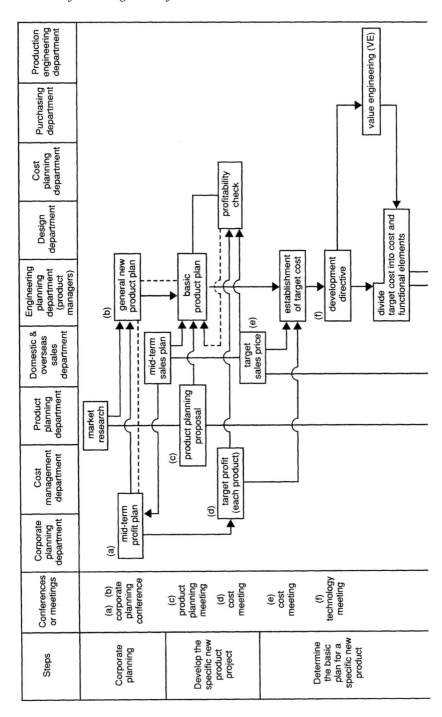

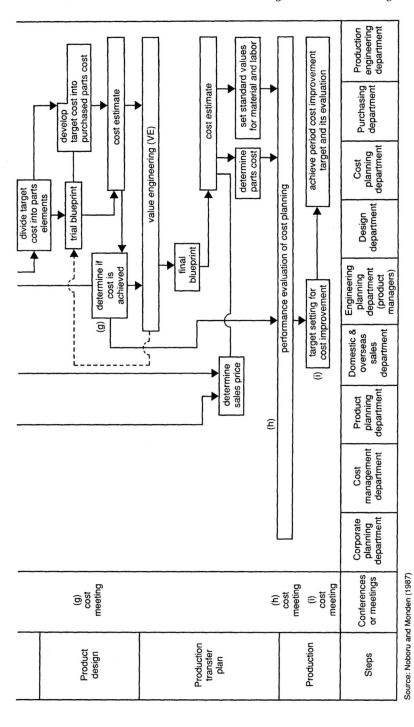

Source: Noboru and Monden (1987)

Figure 2-1. The Target Costing System

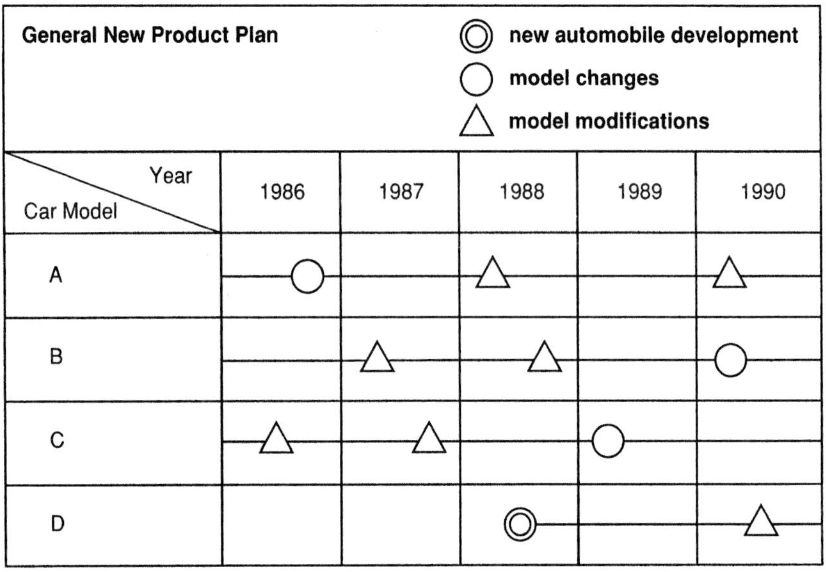

General New Product Plan			◎ new automobile development		
			◯ model changes		
			△ model modifications		

Car Model \ Year	1986	1987	1988	1989	1990
A	◯		△		△
B		△	△		◯
C	△	△		◯	
D			◎		△

Source: Noboru and Monden (1983)

Figure 2-2. General New Product Plan

changes, and model modifications are established for all cars. This plan is illustrated by the form shown in Figure 2-2.

STEP 2: DEVELOPING THE SPECIFIC NEW PRODUCT PROJECT

In order to give shape to the general new product plan, the product planning department presents the engineering planning department with its wishes regarding the type of new product to be developed and the content of the model changes based on market research. This is discussed at the top management product planning meeting and the product planning proposal is prepared. The product manager later gives shape to this plan and establishes the basic product plan.

In this stage, the cost management department estimates the costs of the plan and investigates whether the plan can achieve the target profit. Some automakers use the payback period method as an aid in assessing profitability. The payback period normally covers no more than two model lives; that is, eight years. In the case of a specific facility used exclusively by a certain model, the payback period is usually no more than four years. For a minor model change the period is two years. One major company uses a simple accounting expenses measure (including interest costs) when deciding whether to add facilities. When the project does not appear profitable, the department requests modifications and eliminations. Only the profitable projects are adopted.

STEP 3: DETERMINING THE BASIC PLAN FOR A SPECIFIC NEW PRODUCT

In Step 3, the major cost factors such as design and structure are determined and target costs are established. The product manager requests each department to review material requirements and the manufacturing process, and estimate costs. According to the reports of the departments, the total "estimated cost" is computed.

At the same time, target price figures are gathered from the domestic auto division and the foreign auto division. From these prices and target profit, "allowable cost" is computed. The method of computation is as follows:

Target sales price − target profit = allowable cost

Allowable cost is the cost that top management strongly desires to attain. If this cost is adopted as the target of efforts, the requirement is very severe and not immediately attainable. On the other hand, the estimated cost is not the appropriate target of efforts. Thus, it is necessary to establish a "target cost" that is attainable and motivates employees to make efforts to ultimately achieve the "allowable cost." This is why studies and positive application of motivational factors regarding employee behavior are needed.

Establishing the target cost needs to be reviewed on various dimensions regarding the size of the gap between allowable cost and estimated cost. Once the target cost is determined, and if that plan is approved, top management orders development based on it. Following that, each department implements VE activities regarding the design method in cooperation with each other in order to identify cost effective products that will fulfill customers' demands.

In addition, the engineering planning department decomposes the target cost into each cost element and functional element with the help of the cost management department.[5] Cost elements are material costs, purchased parts costs, direct labor costs, depreciation costs, and so on. Functional elements

Cost Elements / Functions	Material Costs	Purchased Parts Costs	Direct Labor Costs	. . . . .	Total
Engine	$	$	$		$
Transmission System					
Chassis					
(Etc.)					
Total					

The amount should be presented either in the form of the total cost for a single car (in the case of a new model or model change) or as a deviation from the existing model (in the case of model modifications).

Source: Noboru and Monden (1983)

Figure 2-3. Target Cost Broken into Cost Elements and Functions

are engine, transmission system, chassis, and so on. Important points are clarified by these detailed classifications. The form of the classification is shown in Figure 2-3.

The design department also decomposes the target cost into each part. This classification is made to be followed up by target achievement activities in the production design stage including the purchasing department. For this reason, the classification is detailed. The form of the classification is shown in Figure 2-4.

STEP 4: PRODUCT DESIGN

The design department drafts a trial blueprint according to the target cost set for every part. For this draft, information from each department is needed. The design department also actually makes a trial car according to the blueprint and the cost management department estimates its costs.

If there is a gap between the target cost and the estimated cost, the departments execute the VE analysis in cooperation with each other and the trial blueprint is adjusted accordingly. After repeating this process several times, the final blueprint is established.

STEP 5: THE PRODUCTION TRANSFER PLAN

Here, the preparatory condition of production equipment is checked and the cost management department estimates costs according to the final blueprint. The production engineering department establishes standard values of material consumption, labor hours, and so on. Those values are presented to the factory.

Those standard values are used as a data base for computing costs for the purpose of financial accounting and for material requirements planning (MRP). Therefore, they usually are fixed for one year. One major firm calls this value the "basic

Function		Assembly Number					Name						
Major Units	Part Number	Part Name	Quantity	Process	Car Model			Material Cost	Purchased Part Cost	Direct Labor Cost			
					A	B	C			Department	Worker Hours (Minimum)	Amount	
									$	$		$	

Source: Noboru and Monden (1983)

Figure 2-4. Target Cost Broken into Parts Elements

cost." The purchasing department also starts negotiating the prices of purchased parts at this time.

Soon after the target cost is set, production begins. The performance evaluation of target costing then is implemented after new cars have been produced for three months, as abnormal values usually arise during the first three months.

The performance evaluation of target costing is implemented to examine the degree to which the target cost is achieved. If the target cost is not achieved, investigations are made to clarify where the responsibility lies and where the gap arises. These investigations also evaluate the effectiveness of the target costing activities.

These are features of the target costing process used by Japanese automakers. In this process, summarized in Figure 2-5, management accounting plays an important role.

As target costing deals with the development and design of new products, many technical methods of engineering are needed. However, the management accounting system is important in effectively determining target profits, target costs and estimated costs.

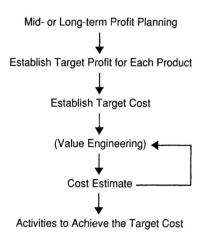

Figure 2-5. Summary of the Target Costing Process

FEATURES OF KAIZEN COSTING

When Japanese accountants hear the words "kaizen costing" they expect a relation to the cost control system based on standard cost accounting. However, kaizen costing in the Japanese automobile industry has not been implemented according to standard costing. This means that the companies do not implement the traditional cost variance analysis based on the gap between the standard cost and the actual cost for each period. Kaizen costing is implemented outside the standard cost system as part of the overall budget control system. In essence, the actual cost per car for the latest period is the kaizen cost budget, which must be reduced in each successive period in order to meet the target profit.

The reason why Japanese automakers implement kaizen costing outside the standard cost accounting system is not because cost reduction in the production stage is taken less seriously, but because it is considered to be very important. Standard costing is limited by its financial accounting purpose in Japanese automobile companies and therefore it has many unsuitable features for cost reduction in the manufacturing phase.

Further, the concept of kaizen costing covers broader meanings than the traditional cost control concept that refers to meeting cost performance standards and to investigating and responding when those standards are not met. Kaizen costing activities include cost reduction activities that require changes in the way the company manufactures existing products. The inadequacy of standard costs for kaizen costing purposes is obvious from the viewpoint of "kaizen" concepts. Also the standard costs are changed only once a year.

Roughly classified, kaizen costing activities are of two kinds. One consists of activities implemented to kaizen actual performance when the difference between actual cost and target cost is large after new products have been in production for three months. The other kind consists of activities implemented continually every period to reduce any difference between target and estimated profit and, thus, to achieve "allowable cost."

In the former case, a special project team called a "cost kaizen committee" is organized and the team implements VE activities. The following distinction between VE and Value Analysis (VA) can be made. VE is the cost reduction activity that involves basic functional changes in the new product development stage. VA is the cost reduction activity that involves design changes of existing products.[6] However, the distinction is not made in this case and the term *VE* is used. Establishing a cost kaizen committee implies that the car model's kaizen is a top priority.

The following is a real life example of activities of the cost kaizen committee. Just after the oil shock in 1973, the profitability of one automobile model showed a marked decrease because of cost increases due to oil. At that time, the plant manager made the following proposals to the top management meeting concerning cost reduction:

1. Establish a cost kaizen committee chaired by the plant manager.
2. Promote a companywide cost reduction program for the specific model.
3. As substructures to this committee, organize the following three subcommittees:
   • production and assembly
   • design and engineering
   • purchasing
4. Establish a cost reduction goal of $75 per automobile.

5. Expect that the previous goal would be achieved within six months.

Through a concerted effect by all departments based on the decisions of the cost kaizen committee, the actual result of the plan was 128 percent attainment of the goal at the end of six months.

The second category of kaizen costing means reaching cost reduction targets established for every department as a result of the short-term profit plan. Different methods are adopted because of the difference between variable and fixed costs. For example, the variable costs such as direct materials, coating, energy, and direct labor costs are managed by setting the amount of kaizen cost per unit of each product type. Fixed costs are subjected to Management by Objectives (MBO) based on the overall amount of kaizen cost instead of the amount of kaizen cost per car.

The purchasing department supervises the purchase prices of parts from outside suppliers. In the factory the most important subject is the use of VE activities to reduce consumption. Usually, the purchasing department is not allocated an amount of kaizen cost target for its own department expenses, but attempts to reduce costs of parts by promoting VE proposals of vendors as well as by negotiating prices with vendors.

As for direct labor costs, monetary control as well as physical control in terms of labor hours is implemented by using the cost decrease amount as the kaizen cost target. A similar approach is applied to material costs improvement.

It is much easier for factory workers to understand the kaizen targets when the amount of cost reduction targets for both fixed and variable costs are presented individually rather than presenting the total cost target. Now we will consider the method of computation for the second category of kaizen costing.

COMPUTING THE TARGET AMOUNT
OF KAIZEN COST

Japanese automakers determine the amount of profit improvement (kaizen profit) based on the difference between target profit (planned by a top-down approach) and estimated profit (computed as a bottom-up estimate). They usually intend to achieve half of that amount by sales increases and half by cost reduction.[7] Of course, when the industry experiences an oil crisis or the high appreciation of currency, greater weight will be imposed on cost reduction.

They reason that the increase in sales increases profit, based partly on the notion of profit contribution. They also reason, based on the idea of ROI, that the sales increases raise the total asset turnover ratio. However, a sales increase can be generated by raising the sales price or increasing sales volume. The former does not cause an increase in variable costs, whereas the latter does.

For generating cost savings, reductions of both variable costs and fixed costs are considered. As most of manufacturing fixed costs are needed for maintaining continuous growth, Japanese automakers generally think that the amount of kaizen cost in the plants should be achieved mainly by reducing variable costs, especially direct material costs and labor costs.

However, in the nonmanufacturing departments, the amount of kaizen cost (or kaizen expense) reduction is set for fixed costs. Departments affected include the head office, research and development, and sales. The design department is usually not assigned an amount of kaizen cost. Also the purchasing department is not assigned one except in special cases such as an oil crisis or a yen appreciation.

The total amount of kaizen costs in all plants, which is (C) in the following formulas, is determined in the cost kaizen meeting as follows:

$$\text{Amount of actual cost per car in last period (A)} = \frac{\text{amount of actual cost in last period} +}{\text{actual production in last period}}$$

$$\text{Estimated amount of actual cost for all plants in this period (B)} = \frac{\substack{\text{amount of actual cost per car in last} \\ \text{period (A)} \times}}{\text{estimated production in this period}}$$

$$\text{Target of kaizen cost in this period = for all plants (C)} \quad \frac{\substack{\text{estimated amount of actual cost for} \\ \text{all plants in this period (B)} \times}}{\substack{\text{target ratio of cost decrease amount} \\ \text{to the estimated cost}}}$$

The target ratio of cost decrease amount to the estimated cost is determined in consideration of attaining the target profit of the year. That ratio is usually around 10 percent. For a new product, the target cost determined in the target costing process is expected to be attained within three months from the time production is started on the new product. After that, the figure can also be reduced further by applying the same technique of kaizen costing.

The target amount of kaizen cost assigned to each factory is as follows:

$$\text{Assignment ratio (D)} = \frac{\text{costs directly controlled by each plant}}{\text{total amount of costs directly by plants}}$$

$$\text{Total amount of kaizen cost for each plant} = \frac{\substack{\text{target of kaizen cost in this period} \\ \text{for all plants (C)} \times}}{\text{assignment ratio (D)}}$$

Cost directly controlled by a plant include direct material costs, direct labor costs, variable overhead costs, and so on. Excluded are the fixed costs such as depreciation costs. The amount of kaizen cost for each plant is decomposed and assigned to each division and that amount is again assigned to smaller units of the organization. Some details about the method of assignment are considered next.

The kaizen cost target is achieved by daily kaizen activities. The JIT production system also intends to reduce various wastes in the plant by these daily activities. Therefore, kaizen costing and the JIT production system are closely related with each other.

KAIZEN COSTING THROUGH "MANAGEMENT BY OBJECTIVES"

Each manufacturing plant has objectives about efficiency, quality, cost, and so on. The concrete targets of physical objectives are determined and evaluated in the production meeting, while kaizen cost targets are determined and evaluated in the kaizen cost meeting.

The cost meetings are held at several organizational levels; for example, at the plant, division, department, section, and process levels. In the meetings for each level, the amount of kaizen cost — that is, the amount of the reduction target — is assigned through Management by Objectives (MBO) at that organizational level.[8] That assignment is called "objectives decomposition" and is implemented according to concrete purposes and policies determined in advance.

However, it is essential that the objectives decomposition not be implemented uniformly, but based on the specifics of each case. Moreover, the determination of each objective, the evaluation, countermeasures, and so on, must be implemented flexibly depending on the specific situation. The outline of objectives decomposition in the plant is shown in Figure 2-6.

Figure 2-7 shows an example of objectives decomposition for attaining the kaizen cost target in a machining

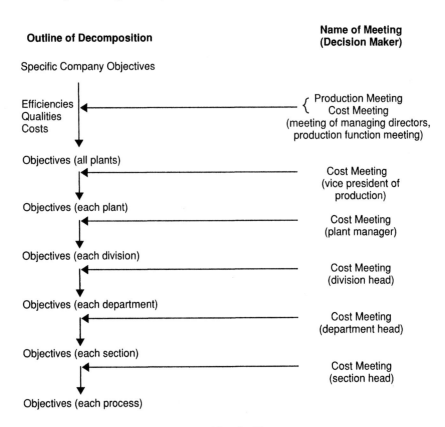

Outline of Decomposition

**Name of Meeting
(Decision Maker)**

Specific Company Objectives

Efficiencies
Qualities
Costs

{ Production Meeting
Cost Meeting
(meeting of managing directors,
production function meeting)

Objectives (all plants)

Cost Meeting
(vice president of
production)

Objectives (each plant)

Cost Meeting
(plant manager)

Objectives (each division)

Cost Meeting
(division head)

Objectives (each department)

Cost Meeting
(department head)

Objectives (each section)

Cost Meeting
(section head)

Objectives (each process)

Figure 2-6. Objectives Decomposition in Plants

department.[9] Figure 2-8 is another example in a stamping department.

In Figure 2-7, managers at each organizational level determine policies and means to attain the kaizen cost target in their department. Their policies and means are mostly non-monetary measures, but the purpose is to realize the kaizen cost target.[10] Managers at each level try to reduce actual labor hours, whereas the accounting department computes the actual labor costs and overhead based on these actual hours. Then actual labor hours and actual labor costs at each organizational level are publicized each month and the result is

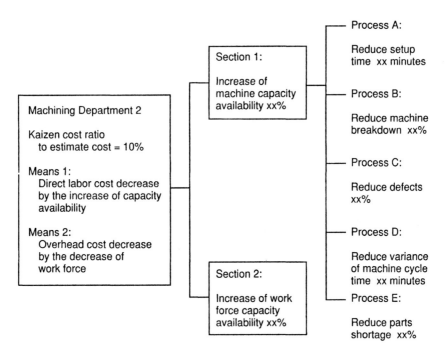

Figure 2-7. Example of Kaizen Cost Decomposition in a Machining Department

reflected via incentive pay in the salaries of the employees. This is quite a motivation. Thus, both production management and accounting control are functioning at the same time in the company.

In the floor-level control activities, the JIT production system has contributed remarkably to the reduction of costs. It is a system that reduces costs by thoroughly excluding waste in plants. Reducing inventories makes managers clarify many problems in plants. If inventories are reduced, the possibility of line-stops arising becomes higher in problematic places. This forces cost reductions by investigating causes of line-stops via defective units, machine breakdowns, and so on.

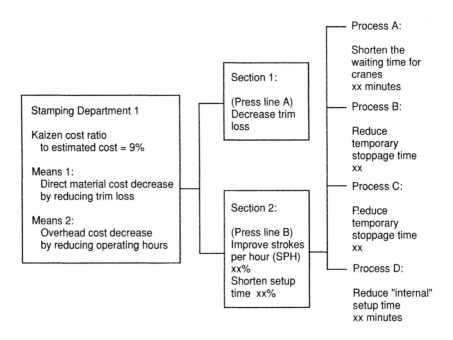

Figure 2-8. Example of Kaizen Cost Decomposition in a Stamping Department

As indicated, through the kaizen costing process, accounting control is used for assigning kaizen cost targets to plants, divisions, departments, and so on. The production and quality control by nonmonetary measures is used for floor-level control activities. On the manufacturing floor, everyone is involved daily in kaizen activities such as QC circles and suggestion systems. Thus, in Japanese automobile companies, accounting controls as well as floor-level controls are integral parts of the kaizen costing process.

MOTIVATIONAL CONSIDERATIONS IN TOTAL COST MANAGEMENT

It is necessary to be aware that target costing may force unreasonable demands on employees. As noted previously, motivational considerations must be considered for the attainability of target costs.

In kaizen costing activities, it is imperative to determine adequately the amount of the kaizen cost target and to assign adequately that amount for each division, department, and so on. It is important that the assignments of the amount are not overly affected by the organizational power structure. Rather, the "self-control" principle (autonomous management by each employee group) should prevail and each target should be determined through consultation between manager and subordinates.

For effective implementation of target costing and kaizen costing, each employee must tackle cost reduction positively. The company needs to devise methods that motivate employees to achieve their targets. Moreover, as VE activities require access to many kinds of information in various departments, methods that promote group activities and cooperation need to be adopted.

As the top row of Figure 2-1 shows, people in all departments are involved in target costing. This includes the purchasing department and suppliers — although the product manager of each model in the engineering planning department assumes major responsibility throughout development and design stages. The product manager plays the role of project leader in a matrix management system. As we also see in Figure 2-6, people in every level of the plant are involved in attaining the kaizen cost target. Thus, *people involvement* is very important in Japanese companies for executing target costing as well as kaizen costing.

SUMMARY

We have considered a total cost management system that includes product development and design activities as well as manufacturing activities. Specifically, we have examined the features of target costing and kaizen costing, which are the primary pillars supporting the total cost management system in all phases of the product life cycle of an automobile.

Although the importance of target costing is currently increasing, kaizen costing should not be slighted. Kaizen costing differs entirely from standard costing in that its goal is the continuous reduction of costs in the manufacturing stage. This is in contrast to standard costing, which aims to achieve and maintain standard costs. Target costing and kaizen costing should be inseparable from one another. If either is ignored, total cost management throughout the whole life of a product cannot be implemented adequately.

CHAPTER THREE

Functional Management to Promote Companywide Coordination: Total Quality Control and Total Cost Management *

TOYOTA'S organization is quite centralized, whereas U.S. motor companies have many decentralized units, called divisions, for each car line which is treated as a profit center. Thus, the responsibility for establishing communication links and coordination between the various departments at Toyota is given to an organizational entity known as a *functional meeting*. Functional meetings do not serve as project teams or task forces. Rather, they are formally constituted, decision-making units whose power cuts across department lines and controls broad corporate functions. Consisting typically of department directors from all parts of the company, each functional meeting will consider such corporate-wide problems as cost management, production management, and quality assurance (QA). The meeting then communicates their policy decisions and plans for

---

* This chapter is a revised version of one appearing in the author's book *Toyota Production System*, 2nd edition, published by the Industrial Engineering and Management Press in Norcross, Georgia. It is reprinted with permission.

implementation to each department for action. Such management through functional meetings is called functional management (*kinohbetsu kanri* at Toyota).

In this chapter, we will examine the structural relationships between the functional meetings and the more formally developed organizations at Toyota, how business policy is made and administered through functional management, and some of the advantages to be gained from the functional management concept. Although the Toyota production system in a narrow sense does not include the product planning and design steps, the author includes functional management in the broad overview of the system. The reader should realize that the most important aspects for increasing productivity or decreasing costs and improving quality are the quality control (QC) and cost reduction activities in the product development and design steps.

Historically, functional management is the outgrowth of a long process of trial and error. The QC Promoting Office at Toyota took the first steps toward companywide QC in 1961 by defining various important functions to be performed by the company. Each department, in turn, collaborated to determine and arrange the contents of the functions. By the addition, integration, and abolition of these inputs, the defined functions were classified and selected into the two most necessary rules for the entire company: quality assurance and cost management. Rules were then established to define what kinds of activities each department must undertake to properly perform these two functions.

QUALITY ASSURANCE

Quality assurance, as defined at Toyota, is to assure that the quality of the product promotes satisfaction, reliability, and economy for the consumer. This rule outlines the activities of each department for quality assurance at all phases from product planning to sales and service. Further, the rule specifies when and what should be assured by whom at where.

The rule defines "when" as eight applicable steps in a series of business activities from planning through sales: product planning, product design, manufacturing preparation, purchasing, manufacturing for sales, inspection, sales and service, and quality audit. The term "by whom at where" means the specific department manager and name of the department. "What" consists of items to be assured and the operations for assurance. Table 3-1 defines the quality assurance rule as it pertains to the steps in the business activities defined here and the primary operations of each department.

COST MANAGEMENT

Toyota utilizes cost management to develop and perform various activities to attain a specific profit goal, evaluate results, and take appropriate action as necessary. In other words, cost management is not simply confined to cost reduction. It also covers companywide activities to acquire profit. This rule specifically outlines the activities of each department level to maintain cost management. The framework of this cost management evolves from the following four categories: cost planning, capital investment planning, cost maintenance, and cost improvement.

Cost planning has been regarded as especially important because most of the cost is determined during development stages of the product. A cost planning manual assigns primary responsibilities and tasks at each phase of product development. Establishing a target cost to be followed during all development stages promotes activities to reduce costs, while maintaining minimum quality standards.

Table 3-1. Quality Assurance Summary

Functional Steps	Person in Charge	Primary Operations for QA	Contribution

Product Planning	• Sales department manager
	• Product planning department head
		1. Forecasts of demands and market share
		2. Obtain the quality to satisfy marketing needs
		  • Set and assign proper quality target and cost target
		  • Prevent recurrence of important quality problems
			△
			
			◎

Product Design	• Design department manager
	• Body-design department manager
	• Engineering department managers
	• Product design department manager
		1. Design prototype vehicles
		  • Meet quality target
		  • Test and examine car for:
		    performance
		    safety
		    low pollution
		    economy
		    reliability
		2. Initial design to confirm necessary conditions for QA
			◎
			○
			
			○

Manufacturing Preparation	• Engineering department managers • QA department manager • Inspection department managers • Manufacturing department manager	1. Prepare overall lines to satisfy design quality 2. Prepare proper inspection methods 3. Evaluate initial prototypes 4. Develop and evaluate a plan of initial and daily process control 5. Prepare line capacities	◎ ○ ○ △ ◎
Purchasing	• Purchasing department managers • QA department manager • Inspection department managers	1. Confirm qualitative and quantitative capabilities of each supplier 2. Inspect initial parts supplied for product quality 3. Support the strengthening of QA system of each supplier	△ △ △
Manufacturing	• Manufacturing department managers • Production control department manager	1. Match product quality to established standards 2. Establish properly controlled lines 3. Maintain necessary line capacities and machine capacities	○ ○ ○
Inspection	• Inspection department manager • QA department manager	1. Inspect initial product for quality 2. Decide whether to deliver product for sale	○ ◎
Sales and Service	• Sales department manager • Export department manager • QA department manager	1. Prevent quality decline in packaging, storage, and delivery 2. Education and public relations 3. Inspect new cars 4. Get feedback and analyze quality information	○ △ △ ◎

Table 3-2. Cost Management Summary

Functional Steps	Related Departments	Cost Management Operations	Contribution
Product Planning	• Corporate planning • Product planning office • Production engineering departments • Accounting departments	1. Set target cost based on new product planning and profit planning, then assign this target cost to various cost factors 2. Set target investment figures 3. Allocate target cost to various design departments of individual parts (cost planning or target costing) 4. Allocate target investment amounts to various investment planning departments (capital budgeting)	◎ ◎ ○ ○
Product Design	• Product planning office • Engineering departments	1. Estimate cost based on prototype drawing 2. Evaluate possibility of attaining target costs 3. Take necessary steps to minimize deviations between target costs and estimated costs through Value Engineering (VE)	◎ ◎ ○
Manufacturing Preparation	• Product planning office • Engineering departments • Manufacturing engineering departments • Production control department	1. Establish cost estimate by considering line preparation and investment plans 2. Evaluate possibility of attaining target costs 3. Take actions to minimize deviations 4. Evaluate facilities investment plans 5. Evaluate production plans, conditions, and decisions to make or buy parts	◎ ◎ ◎ ○ ○
Purchasing	• Purchasing departments	1. Evaluate procurement plans and purchasing conditions 2. Establish control of supplier prices (compare target reduction and actual reduction amounts, analyze variances, and take appropriate action) 3. Investigate improvement of supplier costs [(apply Value Analysis (VA), establish support to promote supplier cost improvement activities)]	○ ○ ◎
Manufacturing Inspection	• Related departments • Accounting department	1. Instigate cost maintenance and improvements (kaizen costing) through the following: • budgeting fixed costs (manufacturing and managerial departments) • cost improvements in primary projects (classified for each type of vehicle and cost factor) • increased cost consciousness of employees through suggestion systems, case presentations, incentive programs, etc.	○ ○ ◎
Sales and Service	• Related departments • Accounting department	1. Measure actual costs of new products through overall evaluation 2. Participate in analyses and discussions at operations check, cost management functional meetings, cost meetings, and various committee meetings	○ ○

Cost maintenance and improvement are cost management processes at the manufacturing level. These are promoted by a companywide budgeting system and the improvement activities described in Chapter 2. To maintain these functions, each department has its own departmental budgeting manual and cost improvement manual.

The contents of cost management activities are specified in detail in the cost management operations assignment manual. Table 3-2 summarizes the cost management rule with respect to related departments and cost management operations.

RELATIONS AMONG DEPARTMENTS, STEPS IN BUSINESS ACTIVITIES AND FUNCTIONS

In order to effectively promote functional management, it must be clearly understood how each step to be performed by each department contributes to its function. Because equal emphasis cannot be placed on all operations, each step must be graded for relative contribution. Thus, the right-hand column in Tables 3-1 and 3-2 describes the relative contribution for each managerial function, as noted by the following symbols:

- ◎ defines factors with critical influence on the function
- ○ defines factors with some influence that could be remedied in later steps
- △ defines factors with relatively small influence

Such assessments were made for all functions. The relationships between departments and functions are summarized in Table 3-3.

The final business purpose at Toyota is to maximize long-range profit under various economic and environmental constraints. This long-range profit will be defined and expressed

Table 3-3. Summary of Various Functional Managements

Business Activity	Related Departments	Functions					
		Quality	Cost	Engineering	Production	Business	Personnel
Product Planning	• Product planning department • Engineering planning department	◎	◎	○	△	◎	○
Product Design	• Laboratory • Design department	◎	○	◎	○	○	○
Manufacturing Preparation	• Manufacturing engineering department • Manufacturing planning department	◎	◎	○	◎	△	○
Purchasing	• Purchasing department • Purchasing management department	◎	◎	△	△	△	○
Manufacturing	• Motomachi plant • Honsha plant	◎	○	△	◎	○	◎
Sales	• Sales department • Export department	◎	○	○	○	◎	○

Departmental Management

Functional Management

as a concrete figure through long-range business planning. Therefore, each function must be selected carefully and organized to be helpful in attaining the long-range profit.

If the number of functions was too high, then each function would begin to interfere with other functions, frustrating attempts to produce a new product in a timely and cost effective manner. Further, too many functions will foster strong independence of certain functions to the point that each departmental management might be enough to perform the function.

Conversely, if the number of functions was too small, too many departments would be related in a single function. Managing so many departments from a certain functional standpoint would be very complicated, if not impossible.

Toyota regards quality assurance and cost management as paramount functions, or *purpose functions*, and calls them the two pillars of functional management. Other functions are regarded as *means functions*. Thus, product planning and product design are integrated into an engineering function; manufacturing preparation and manufacturing into a production function; and sales and purchasing into a business function.

As a result, six functions remain in the Toyota functional management system, as illustrated in Table 3-3. In summary, each function in new product development, manufacturing technique, and marketing philosophy is not identical with other functions in its character or priority.

ORGANIZATION OF THE FUNCTIONAL MANAGEMENT SYSTEM

At Toyota, each director of the company is responsible for a certain department. Since each department involves more than one function, each director must participate in multiple functions, as we see in Table 3-3. No single director is responsible for a single function; he or she serves as a member of a team. Conversely, not all department directors participate in all functions. This would create difficulties managing each functional meeting because of too many members. For example, although there are thirteen departments involved in product planning and product design, only one or two directors will attend a QA functional meeting.

As previously stated, the functional meeting is the only formal organizational unit in functional management. Each functional meeting is a chartered decision-making unit charged to plan, check, and decide remedial actions required to achieve a functional goal. Each individual department serves as a line unit to perform the actions dictated by the functional meeting.

Figure 3-1 details the framework of the top management organization at Toyota. Each department is managed by a managing director or common director, whereas each functional meeting consists of all directors, including six executive directors. Since each executive director is responsible for integrating the actions of various departments, he or she will participate as chairperson in those functional meetings that have close relationships with that executive director's integrated departments. By necessity, even a vice president may participate in a functional meeting. A functional meeting typically numbers about ten members.

The QA and cost management functional meetings are conducted once a month. Generally, other functional meetings are held every other month. A functional meeting should not be convened without a significant agenda.

Functional meetings are positioned below the management meeting which consists of all managing directors and the standing auditor. The management meeting is an executive organization that gives final approval to the decisions of

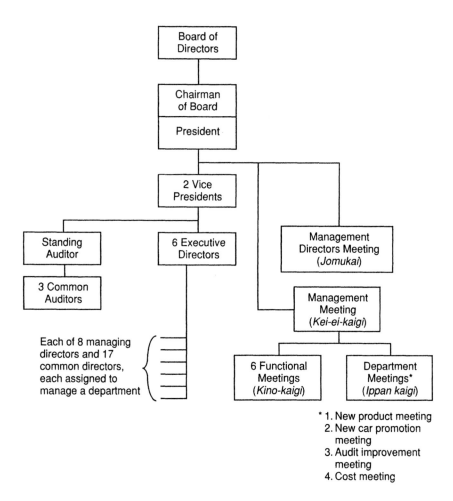

Figure 3-1. Framework of Toyota Management Organization (as of 1981)

the functional meeting. However, the essential decision-making authority remains with each functional meeting because implementation of the decision begins at the functional meeting. As long as there are no special objections in the management meeting, the decision made by the functional meeting will be treated as a company decision.

The *departmental meetings* shown in Figure 3-4 provide each department with a vehicle to discuss implementation of decisions made by the functional meeting. Note that the departmental meeting is not positioned as a substructure of the functional meeting. As with the functional meetings, plans for implementation generated within departmental meetings are subject to review and approval by the management meeting.

Occasionally, a problem arises such as a need to achieve a certain quality characteristic within a short-term period that cannot be resolved by only one functional meeting. By necessity, labor hours and costs must increase to improve the quality. At this time, a *joint functional meeting* combines quality and production functions. Further, in order to cope with a new legal restriction for safety and pollution, most of the functions, such as QA, cost, engineering, and production, must consider the restriction together. In this case, an *enlarged functional meeting* is formed to consider the problem. Note that these are not permanent organizational entities.

Another example involves a *cost management functional meeting*. Just after the oil shock in 1973, the profitability of the Toyota Corolla showed a marked decrease because of cost increases due to oil prices. At that time, the plant manager of Corolla made the following proposals to the cost functional meeting:

1. Promote a companywide cost reduction movement for Corolla.
2. Organize a Corolla Cost Reduction Committee chaired by the plant manager.
3. As substructures to this committee, organize the following sectional meetings:
    • production and assembly
    • design and engineering
    • purchasing

4. Establish a cost reduction of $40 per automobile.
5. Achieve the goal within six months.

Through a concerted effort by all departments based on the decisions of the cost management functional meeting, the actual result of the plan was 128 percent attainment of the goal at the end of six months (May 1975).

BUSINESS POLICY AND FUNCTIONAL MANAGEMENT

Since the introduction of the CWQC concept, a business policy has been developed and published. The policy applies to the operations level and includes each function previously discussed. The six elements of the business policy are shown in Figure 3-2 and defined in the following sections.

FUNDAMENTAL POLICY   Fundamental policy is the business ethic principle, or fundamental directions, of the company. Once established, it will not change for many years.

An example is "Toyota wishes to develop in the world by collecting all powers inside and outside the company." The expression is abstract, but represents a business philosophy of top management. The fundamental policy is used to guide long-range planning.

LONG-TERM GOALS   Long-term goals are goals to be attained within five years as an output of long-range planning. These goals are concrete figures expressed for production quality, sales quality, market share and return on investment (ROI), and so on.

LONG-TERM POLICY   Long-term policy is the strategy used to achieve the long-term goals, and is expressed in more concrete detail than the fundamental policy. It covers several items common to the overall company.

For example: "In order to manage the overall company in a scientific manner, policies, goals, and plans must be prepared for each department and a control point must be defined clearly and directed."

ANNUAL SLOGANS Annual slogans are a means for Toyota to emphasize annual policies. The purpose of these slogans is to encourage a sound mental attitude in all employees and there are two types.

The first type remains the same every year, such as "Assure the quality in every Toyota." The second type emphasizes the policy for the year. For example, the 1974 slogan after the oil shock was "Build Toyotas for the changing age." Also: "It is time to use scarce resources effectively."

ANNUAL GOALS OF EACH FUNCTION Accepting the long-term goals just described, the annual goals of each function to be achieved within the current year must be expressed in specific figures. These goal figures are established for each function. Each functional meeting, in turn, decides how to achieve these goals. The items included as annual goals for each function follow:

- *Overall Company:* ROI, production quantity, and market share
- *Production:* rate of reduced manpower to previous year's manpower level
- *Quality:* rate of reduction of problems in the marketplace
- *Cost:* total amount of costs to be reduced, plant and equipment investment amount, and margin rates of the preferentially developed automobiles
- *Safety, sanitation, and environment:* number of closures for holidays, and so on, at business and plants

ANNUAL WORKING PLANS OF EACH FUNCTION
Once annual goals are established for each function, annual working plans of each function must be determined by the appropriate functional meeting. Implementation of these working plans then becomes the responsibility of the department meeting.

Classification of the functions shown in Figure 3-2 differs somewhat from that presented in Table 3-3 because the business policy must describe all the important topics to be achieved in the current year. The business function in Table 3-3 is incorporated into the overall company function shown in Figure 3-2, which also includes information and public relations. Further, although the safety, sanitation, and environment functions are not shown in Table 3-3, nor is there a functional meeting, safety and environment are included

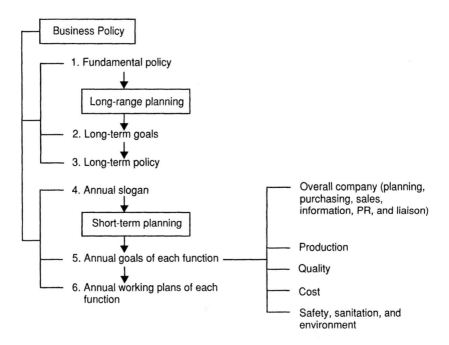

Figure 3-2. Six Elements of Business Policy at Toyota

with the production functional meeting, while sanitation is included with both the production and personnel functions.

EXTENSION OF BUSINESS POLICY

Formal announcement of the business policy at Toyota is made by the president in his New Year's greetings to the employees. Extension plans of each function are issued to each department by the office of the functional meeting. Department policies and plans then are formulated by the department meeting.

After implementation of these plans, the results of actual performance are evaluated during the middle and at the end of the current year. Feedback from these evaluations are used to form the policies for the next year. Such checks and evaluations are made at three levels within the organization: operations checks of selected topics by top management, functional checks by each functional meeting chairperson, and department checks by each department manager or director. Figure 3-3 shows the organization planning and control system employed at Toyota.

CRITICAL CONSIDERATIONS FOR FUNCTIONAL MANAGEMENT

Four critical considerations demand special attention in order to achieve a successful functional management program:

1. Select important functions carefully to properly balance department participation. Too many departments in the same functional meeting lead to confusion and difficulties managing the meeting. Too few member departments create a need for many individual functions that will begin to overlap responsibilities, again creating confusion and management problems.

2. Do not regard functional management as an informal system. The position and guidelines of functional

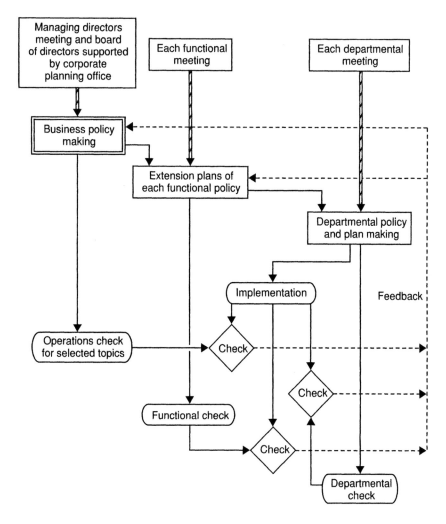

Figure 3-3. Toyota Planning and Control System

meetings in the top management scheme must be
defined clearly. The functional meeting must receive
the necessary authority to implement its decisions as
company policy.

3. Each line department must have a strong structure in place to execute the plans put forth by the various meetings.
4. The director in charge of each function is also the head of a department. This individual, however, must formulate and direct the function for the overall company, not for a particular department.

ADVANTAGES OF FUNCTIONAL MANAGEMENT

Functional management as implemented at Toyota offers certain advantages not found in other management systems. For example:

- Both policies and implementation are decisive and rapidly instituted. This results because the functional meeting is a substantive decision-making entity with responsibilities and authority directed from top management. In addition, communication to executing line departments is rapid since members of the functional meeting are also directors responsible for related departments.
- *Nemawashi* is unnecessary at Toyota. The original meaning of this term comes from the preparations for transplanting a large tree. One must dig around the roots, cutting larger ones so that smaller roots run to secure its new position. In business, *nemawashi* refers to the persuasion of related individuals, such as management executives, prior to a formal decision-making meeting. At Toyota, the functional meeting itself becomes the *nemawashi* negotiation.
- Functional meetings serve to enhance communications and human relations among the various depart-

ments because all sides are brought together to achieve a common goal.

- Communications from subordinate employees to the functional meetings are achieved easily because there is no need for prior persuasion. Employees bring their suggestions and ideas to their department managers for discussion at the functional meetings.

—————

CHAPTER 4

Flat Organizational
and Personnel Management

IN RECENT YEARS, diversifying customer needs, technological progress, internationalization, and other trends have created a fast-changing business environment to which companies must learn to respond flexibly and swiftly.

Company organizations can respond effectively to the needs of this changing environment in two ways:

The first is by accelerating the decision-making process; that is, the events that occur between recognizing the need for a decision and establishing the final decision. We call the time period for these events the "decision-making lead time." If a company can shorten its decision-making lead time, it is then better able to (1) take advantage of new business opportunities, (2) carry out more timely new product development, and (3) respond more promptly and effectively to any customer complaints that arise. We can think of this type of improvement as implementing the just-in-time approach within the decision-making process.

Second, companies should cultivate among employees an ambition to accept challenges. In many cases, popular products result from a company organization that encourages younger, freer-thinking employees to be assertive in proposing their own ideas. It is especially important for companies in mature or declining industries to give free rein to employee ingenuity in developing ideas for new fields of business.

This chapter studies the various methods that Toyota uses to speed up its decision-making process and cultivate the challenging employee talents and abilities, enabling the company to respond more flexibly and swiftly to our fast-changing business environment. The following observations should help make us more conscious of just how important and universal this new theme in organizational management is for companies today.

In Figure 4-1, I have outlined the reforms that Toyota has made recently in its corporate organization and personnel system. We will examine these reforms one by one in order.

ACCELERATING THE DECISION-MAKING PROCESS THROUGH REORGANIZATION

On August 1, 1989, Toyota implemented a new organization structure. The principle objective of this reorganization was to speed up the decision-making process.[1] This new organization did away with the traditional pyramid structure of middle-management ranks and replaced it with a flatter structure that has fewer layers and is centered on offices within each department that are supervised by only two layers: office chiefs and the department chief. (See Figure 4-2.)

Prior to this reorganization, Toyota's middle management included numerous layers that included the department chief, deputy department chief, supervisors, section chiefs, assistant section chiefs, and chief clerks. There are now only three layers — department chief, office chiefs, and group leaders.

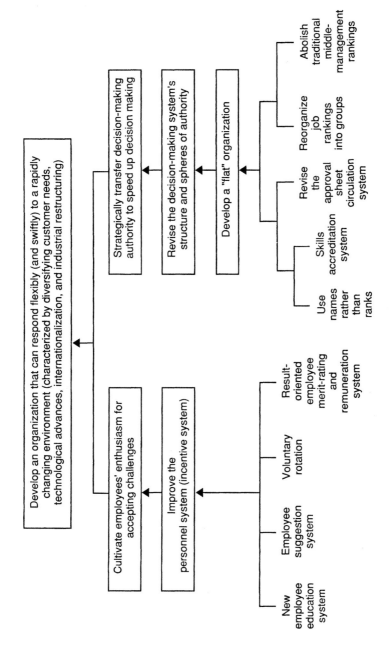

Figure 4-1. Reforms to Accelerate Decision-making

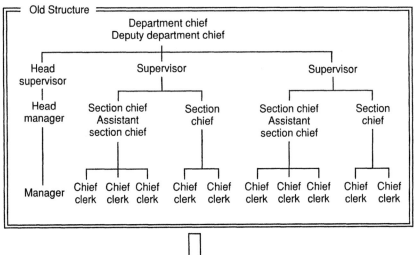

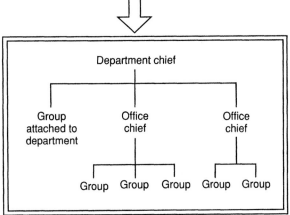

Figure 4-2. Reorganization of Middle Management at Toyota

In addition to reducing the number of layers in the middle-management structure, the new "office-based" structure consolidates what used to be two or three departments into each office. The groups in these offices are able to reorganize themselves with flexibility whenever such regrouping is deemed necessary by the department chief. Membership in these groups is open to a wide range of people, from department chiefs to ordinary employees.

The only type of group whose position has yet to be defined clearly is the "group attached to department" type shown in Figure 4-2.

Toyota implemented this organizational reform in all of its clerical and engineering departments except for those in overseas offices and in plant-based production departments. As a result, some 20,000 of Toyota's roughly 67,000 employees were directly affected by this reorganization.

From my own perspective, I find the following advantages in switching from a multi-layered pyramid structure to this simpler and flatter structure.

1. It speeds up the decision-making process by streamlining the approval sheet circulation system (the *ringi* system) to reduce both the number of managers at each rank and the number of managerial ranks that receive the approval sheet.

2. Decision-making authority is no longer spread so far vertically and horizontally in the management structure but is restricted instead to group leaders and their superiors. Clearly defined guidelines have been created to regulate the transfer of authority.

3. The number of middle-management positions has been reduced by about half, which makes it easier for lower-level employees to get their ideas across to top managers. In other words, it creates in a more streamlined and direct course for the bottom-up flow of information in the company. As a result, younger employees are encouraged to propose ideas to their higher-ups.

4. Requests and complaints from customers also travel more easily through the organizational ranks to top management. This helps Toyota live up to its "customers first" philosophy.

5. Upper-level managers used to spend a lot of time supervising the various ranks of middle managers and

had little opportunity to develop specific skills. The new group-based structure enables the managers and employees of individual groups to develop higher levels of knowledge and technical skill thus raising the quality of their own work.

While the number of people in one office may range from thirty to one hundred, the average office is made up of about fifty people. Their work includes routine work, strategic work, and work based on various types of project themes, both large and small.

The new rank of office chief, while primarily made up of former supervisors, include former department chiefs and section chiefs. The group leaders, while mostly former section chiefs, also include some assistant department chiefs and chief clerks. The people selected for specific project themes represent a wide range of backgrounds and qualifications.

To maintain this new organization's flexibility and enthusiasm, the personnel department promotes close communication among department chiefs, office chiefs, and other managers, and downplays rank status as a barrier to such communication.

All together, there were some 6,200 department chiefs, deputy department chiefs, section chiefs, and chief clerks whose ranks were changed by this reorganization.

The number of departments at Toyota increased slightly, from 173 before the reorganization to 177 afterward. While the number of departments did not change much, the number of sections was reduced by two-thirds and lower management positions within the sections were cut by about half. The group leaders were the most active rank in the decision-making process. The number of section chiefs and chief clerks, who traditionally had more passive roles, fell from about 2,000 persons to a little over 1,000.

In addition, Toyota made other department-level organizational changes that broadened employee training to include hiring, job assignment, benefits, and training to develop an organization better able to respond to international operations in various countries.[2] Toyota reorganized both the personnel and education departments, renaming the latter the human resources development department. It then established a third department called the international personnel department.

Another new department established at this time was the Motor Sports Department, whose main purpose is to boost Toyota's activities in motor sports and to help promote the company's technological development.

CHANGES IN THE APPROVAL SHEET SYSTEM

In August 1988, exactly one year before the organizational changes described above were made, Toyota launched what it called a three stamp campaign. Until then, approval sheets concerning management decisions had required seven or eight different people to sign off by affixing their name stamps *(hanko)*. Developers of the campaign found that the number of people who need to receive such approval sheets could be reduced responsibly to just three, hence the name for their improvement scheme. Gradually, this campaign became a means to prepare for the major organizational changes of the following year. The three stamp campaign had the following three goals:

1. Speed up the decision-making process.
2. Train lower-ranked managers by delegating more responsibility to their areas.
3. Improve morale.

The following describes some of the advantages and disadvantages of the conventional approval sheet system.[3]

Because the conventional approval sheet system tended to concentrate authority in the upper management ranks, Toyota found it difficult to delegate more authority to middle and lower managers.

As more items require approval sheets, less authority (and, therefore, less responsibility) is given to section chiefs and other lower-ranked managers. In many cases, if the decision has poor results, responsibility for the mistake does not stop with the high-ranked person on the approval sheet but extends to the person or persons who proposed the decision in the first place. When the managers who need to sign off are many and spread among several departments or management levels, it tends to take longer to reach a consensus in approving the decision.

Under the *flat organization* scheme, Toyota has aimed to reduce the number of items that require approval sheets while also reducing the variety (ranks) and number of managers who must receive the sheets.

The three stamp campaign has helped clarify the decision-making criteria for each level of management at Toyota. By decision-making criteria, we mean such matters as who has the right to propose decisions, who such decision items must be submitted to for approval, and who has the final decision-making authority.

However, even streamlining the approval sheet system leaves a number of problems. For instance, the following three problems relate to the budgeting system.[4]

INADEQUATE DELEGATION OF AUTHORITY

For example, a sales section chief is given a certain amount of freedom, within the budgeted allowance, to charge the company for client entertainment expenses. Although the section chief generally is responsible for how the budgeted expense allowance is spent, he or she needs the division chief's approval for any expense items that exceed the per-item cost ceiling — and therefore does not have full authority over the expense account.

ITEMS OUTSIDE OF BUDGET

This type of problem exists in any kind of budgeting system, whether or not it follows the conventional approval system format. *Items outside of budget* refers to expense items that were not anticipated when the budget was planned. Such items must be approved separately via some kind of special-case approval system. Alternatively, they can be handled by a committee whose responsibilities specifically include the formal processing of items outside of budget.

ITEMS THAT REQUIRE SPECIAL TREATMENT

As an example, plant investment budgets generally allocate a certain amount of funds for the year. However, often it is uncertain what kinds of projects will be claiming some of these funds in the year's third and/or fourth quarter. When deciding upon such projects, the managers responsible for planning them must submit approval sheets and receive prior approval from higher-ups. Other types of major expense items that may require similar special treatment include major repair schemes and sales publicity campaigns. Generally, it may be a good idea to have an approval sheet system for certain activities (such as publicity campaigns), when those activities are initially given a very loose budget framework to work within. This would help activity planners be more flexible in responding to current conditions.

SKILLS ACCREDITATION SYSTEM AND USE OF NAMES INSTEAD OF RANKS

Although the implementation of the new flat organization did away with certain management ranks such as section chief and chief clerk, those job titles are still being used in the skills accreditation system.

At Toyota, all promotions, salaries, and job titles for use outside the company are based on the individual's skills accreditation level and not on his or her current job assignment.

Toyota had introduced its skills accreditation system in November 1987. This system had established skill levels called councillor, vice councillor, and competent authority. However, when the flat organization was established, the skill level titles were changed to department chief class, supervisor class, section chief class, chief clerk class, and so on.

On the business cards for presentation to customers and other outside contacts, the managers who have reached the section chief class in the skills accreditation system are identified as "chief of XXX section, XXX department." Likewise, those who have reached the chief clerk level in skills accreditation are described as "chief clerk of XXX section, XXX department." In other words, even though there are no longer any of the old multilayered sections in the organization, the company has retained the old section-based titles for formal purposes — such as on business cards.

Why bother with such formalities? Mainly, it is for the sake of convenience. Japanese society is still a rank-oriented society, and if Toyota's managers were to dispense with the traditional management rankings, they would find it more difficult to assure their customers and other contacts outside the company of their position and authority within Toyota.

Meanwhile, internally Toyota is trying to become less rank-oriented. This is not only by introducing the new flat organization, but also by encouraging employees to address their higher-ups by their names (for example, Mr. Yamada or Ms. Aoki) instead of by their rank, which has been the custom. This was done to help the new flat organization achieve one of its goals — to make it easier for lower-level managers to get their ideas across to higher-ups, especially in view of the fact that it is often the younger employees who have the original ideas for new hit products.

As such, this new way of addressing managers recognizes that a flat organization alone will not improve the decision-making process much if there still exists an atmosphere that stifles the free expression of ideas. In addition, the act of changing customs by calling managers by their names helps employees to change their way of thinking about the organization. It helps them feel personally involved in the reform process.

It has been suggested, however, that the retention of traditional ranks for use outside the company dampens this new, reform-minded way of thinking.[5] Such critics point out that ordinary employees find it difficult to ignore a person's ranking when the employee knows that person still carries a traditional ranking, at least on his or her business card.

In any case, one would have to admit that it is not very easy to buck tradition and establish a new mode for human relationships.

REFORMING THE PERSONNEL SYSTEM TO CULTIVATE THE CHALLENGING EMPLOYEE

Despite the previously described factors that were designed to help employees change their way of thinking, simply changing the structure of an organization is rarely enough to revitalize the organization. Instead, a new system must be established that inspires people within the organization to get personally involved in its revitalization.

As mentioned earlier, today's business environment is one in which companies must come up with fresh ideas that meet with diversifying customer needs. At the same time, companies must maintain a forward-thinking R&D program to keep pace with rapidly advancing high technologies and developing employee skills, both to meet the challenges of corporate internationalization and overseas operations and to develop and promote ideas for new business ventures.

The term *incentive systems* is used to describe systems that are designed to promote employee enthusiasm and confidence in accepting these kinds of challenges. Toyota has introduced the following four incentive systems:[6]

1. a personnel merit-rating and compensation system to emphasize results
2. voluntary rotation
3. an in-house suggestion system for recruiting
4. a new employee education system

The previous personnel merit-rating system, which had been based on seniority and accumulated merit, was changed to emphasize the evaluation of job performance in recent months and years. In addition, the previous overall evaluation system was made more specific by dividing evaluation into (1) merit during the past year (reflected in the size of the two semiannual bonuses), which looks at what kinds of projects have been undertaken and the results achieved, and (2) skill merit based on what specialist skills the employee has worked toward mastering (reflected in promotions to higher ranks).

Currently, the higher-ranked employees generally evaluate their subordinates in terms of factors such as job performance, character, and teamwork skills. In April 1990, a new job performance evaluation method was added to this same general evaluation method. It entails that once yearly each employee meets with his or her superior to discuss and establish job performance targets. At the end of the business year, they meet again to evaluate job performance in reaching the targets set for that year.

In determining the size of employee salaries, Toyota applies these job performance evaluation results as 10 percent of the total evaluation score, while a higher percentage is applied to determining bonuses. This means that job performance now plays a direct role in assessing employee remuneration in terms of semiannual bonuses.[7] Toyota has applied this new assessment system to all of its clerical and research departments. The new system's mechanism of assessing employee remuneration based partly on achieving job performance targets has made everyone aware of a new emphasis on skills and results.

As for voluntary rotation, Toyota employees who have been working in the same department or section for at least five years are able to apply for transfer (rotation) to their preferred department. Generally, the company is able to accommodate the employee's rotation request within two years. As such, this system supports employees' desires to pursue the job challenges that interest them most.

With the in-house suggestion system, Toyota actively seeks out employee ideas as the company considers expanding into promising new fields of business, such as motor sports and leisure-related businesses. Also employees who want to promote new businesses are invited to remain with the company.

In February 1989, Toyota established a *business development office* to promote new business expansion outside its main business. In May 1989, all managers ranked at the section chief level or higher were asked to submit suggestions for new business ideas. This campaign generated some 700 suggestions.

In broad terms, Toyota's new employee education system relates to the company's entire organizational reform program.

Specifically, however, it relates to efforts to promote educational exchanges with companies in other industries to help broaden and deepen specialist skills among managers.

IMPROVING THE OFFICE ENVIRONMENT — LAYOUT IMPROVEMENT

In 1990, Toyota adopted a three-year plan to invest roughly ¥ 5 billion per year to improve the work environment in its offices.[8] Intended to help reinvigorate the organization, this campaign was launched as part of a program to reevaluate various office facilities, raise the operational efficiency in offices, and boost employee morale.

Toyota already had begun the same program on an experimental basis in August 1988 at its head office (Toyoda City, Aichi Prefecture) and at other offices, including its Tokyo branch office (Bunkyo-ku, Tokyo) and its North America office. This experimental program proved successful, which led Toyota to implement it companywide.

Specifically, in August 1988 Toyota changed the layout of its personnel department offices located on the fifth floor of the No. 1 head office building. In the new layout, the desk of the chief personnel officer (Director Isomura) was placed in the center of the large (about 840 square meters) main floor. The desks of the various department and office chiefs were placed around it, followed by rows of the other employee desks.

Compared to the previous layout, which had executives' desks lined up along the sides of the room with lower-ranked employees' desks sandwiched in the middle, the lower-ranked employees preferred the improved layout. They felt it was easier for them to communicate. In addition, some of the conventional rectangular desks were replaced with more stylish round or oval desks, and the office automation equipment was upgraded.

EMPLOYEES' EVALUATION OF TOYOTA'S PERSONNEL ORGANIZATION REFORMS

The following information was taken from the responses to a questionnaire that Toyota circulated among some of its employees to determine how well its major organizational and personnel system reforms were accepted.[9]

The questionnaire asked participants to evaluate the organizational reforms. It was circulated among 2,500 randomly selected employees ranked from ordinary employee to department chief. Questionnaire results were announced on November 11, 1989.

Roughly 70 percent of the department chiefs (about 500 people) felt that the new flat organization gave more decision-making authority to their subordinates. Meanwhile, 60 percent of all respondents felt their way of working had changed as a result of the reforms. Likewise, 60 percent of all respondents reported that they had followed the suggestion of the campaign to downplay rank and had begun calling managers by their names instead of their rank. In addition, about 80 percent of all respondents said they were implementing the new policy of requiring only three name stamps on approval sheets as recommended by the three stamp campaign.

These results assured Toyota's top managers that their organizational reforms were a success.

CONCLUSION

The major organizational and personnel system reforms undertaken by Toyota have removed, with surgical precision, much of the fat and lethargy that is symptomatic of the large corporation syndrome. As a result, the traditional pyramid-shaped organizational structure has been flattened out considerably, with more decision-making authority accorded to middle- and lower-management people, while making it easier for everyone, including the youngest employees, to communicate their ideas assertively to superiors. All of these changes have helped make Toyota's organization more efficient, flexible, and energetic in its responses to today's rapidly changing environment.

CHAPTER 5

Sales Management System

The sales volume and market share of any particular product is determined by the product's sales strength and the company's sales strength.

In considering the product's sales strength, the most important factor is how well the product's developers have anticipated user trends such as changing social conditions and lifestyles. Sometimes, a single product has enough sales strength to pull its company from behind into the lead against the competition. This happened in Japan when Asahi Breweries marketed its "Super Dry" beer and when Nissan introduced its "Cima" line of luxury cars. We will study Toyota's new product development system in Chapter 6.

As for the company's sales strength, the prime determinant of sales volume is the number of sales outlets and the number of salespeople. This can be termed the company's quantitative sales strength. However, it is also important to consider how powerful each sales outlet's sales activities are; in other words, how stimulated and energized the staff at each sales office is by the challenge of taking on the competition. This we call the company's qualitative sales strength.

In this chapter we will examine the key factors behind Toyota's quantitative and qualitative sales strengths, focusing on the characteristics of Toyota's sales network and sales channels.

CHARACTERISTICS OF TOYOTA'S SALES NETWORK

QUANTITATIVE STRENGTH

The secret of Toyota's powerful sales network lies in its massive size and its high quality, both of which are the legacy of a Mr. Shōtarō Kamiya.

Toyota Motor was born from a loom manufacturing company known as Toyoda Automatic Loom Works. This company began trial production of passenger cars in 1934.* In October 1935, company president Kiichirō Toyoda lured Shōtarō Kamiya away from Nippon GM and gave him the job of marketing Toyota's new cars. Later, when Toyota split into the manufacturing company Toyota Motor Company and the sales company Toyota Motor Sales, Kamiya was installed as the latter company's president, and was so successful that he earned the nickname "the god of sales." When Kamiya quit Nippon GM to join Toyota, he brought along two of his subordinates: Shikanosuke Hanazaki and Taneyuki Kato. Kamiya also managed to talk several of Nippon GM's Chevrolet and Buick sales outlets into switching over to the Toyota Group.

Meanwhile, Nissan followed Toyota's lead two years later by recruiting Sadajiro Ashida from Nippon GM to help establish Nissan Auto Sales. Since Toyota had already picked through the GM dealers for converts, Nissan approached Ford dealers about joining the Nissan group, but had little

---

* In Japanese, the family name "Toyoda" means "abundant rice field." In 1936 a contest was held to choose a more marketable name for the new automobiles — and "Toyota" was chosen.

success. From that time on, Nissan clearly lagged behind Toyota in terms of sales strength.

Kamiya's basic policy concerning sales outlets was to follow Ford and GM's lead in establishing one dealer franchise per prefecture. In addition, Kamiya worked to establish a network of independent specialist sales outlets to be set up using local capital and local citizenry. These policies remain fundamental to Toyota's sales network even today.

President Kamiya once remarked that the reason Toyota was able to lure away so many of Nippon GM's sales outlets was because these sales outlets resented Nippon GM because of its failure to use local capital and its single-minded pursuit of big profits. He felt that the proper relationship between car manufacturers and dealers should be one of mutual prosperity. This sales philosophy still lives at Toyota. It is safe to say that a company that follows an excellent business philosophy is best assured of success and prosperity.

These developments eventually led to the founding of Toyota Motor Company in August 1937.

During World War II, automobiles came under a rationing system established by the wartime government. In 1942, the Nippon Automobile Distribution Company *(Nippon Jidosha Haikyu Kabushiki Kaisha)* was established. Known as *Nichihai* for short, this company established regional affiliates called regional automobile distribution companies *(chiho jidosha haikyu kabushiki kaisha)*, or *Jihai* for short, that grouped together car dealers belonging to the various manufacturers' groups. The military had first pick of all automobiles that left the nation's factories. Nichihai then bought up whatever inventory was left over and distributed the vehicles to the various Jihai companies. They in turn sold them to private-sector buyers. Kamiya was assigned to Nichihai as a managing director in charge of the vehicle division.

The postwar Ministry of Transport dissolved the Nichihai/Jihai network in June 1946, and authorized the reestablishment of the manufacturer sales networks that had existed prior to the war. At that time, the reborn Toyota Group welcomed back the able salespeople who had run their sales outlets earlier. In addition, Toyota managed to win over several former Nissan salespeople.

It is no exaggeration to say that the current domestic share gap between Toyota and Nissan began during that decisive period in postwar Japan. During the war, Kamiya made it clear to the other Nichihai leaders that sales people depended upon demand and manufacturers depended upon sales people. This philosophy was enshrined in Kamiya's famous dictum: *The customer comes first, the dealer second, and the manufacturer third.* This was the type of thinking that attracted so many dealers to Toyota when the new dealership groups were reestablished. In a sense, Kamiya already had dealt a decisive blow to his competitors even before the battle began.

In this way, Toyota outperformed the competition and, as of 1988, accumulated 4,333 sales outlets, staffed by some

Table 5-1. Sales Forces of Major Japanese Automakers

	Sales Companies	Sales Outlets	No. of Salespeople
Toyota	314	4,333	40,600
Nissan	243	3,020	28,000
Mazda	111	1,589	12,000
Mitsubishi	333	1,296	9,000
Honda	1,610*	2,260	7,600

* This figure includes 1,400 "Primo" companies. Other industry estimates for number of salespeople: 5,000 for Daihatsu, 3,500 for Fuji Heavy Industries (Subaru), and 3,300 for Suzuki Motors.

40,600 well-trained salespeople. Compare this to 28,000 sales-people for Nissan and 12,000 for Mazda.

As shown in Table 5-1, the expansion of Toyota's sales network did not happen in sudden leaps and bounds. Rather, much of it resulted directly from the diligent and well-timed efforts of Kamiya over a period of many years. This kind of expansion is not subject to the sudden reversals of fortune that can be seen in product sales strength. The key to Toyota's steady sales network expansion over the past few decades has been an emphasis not only on increasing the number of sales outlets and sales staff but also on enriching and strengthening these outlets by providing excellent guidance and training.

EXCLUSIVE DEALERSHIP AND TERRITORY SYSTEM

All of Japan's automakers have established a franchise system based on exclusive dealerships and territories. The first to build such a system was Toyota, under the leadership of Shōtarō Kamiya.

The exclusive dealerships have the following features:

- The manufacturer markets its products exclusively through sales companies (dealerships) that handle only that manufacturer's products.
- The manufacturer forbids the dealerships from handling any other manufacturer's products.
- The manufacturer ensures that the dealership is the sole agency for the manufacturer's products within a certain area.

The territory system has the following features:

- The manufacturer defines the borders of each dealership's sales territory.

- Dealership sales territories can be defined either as closed territories, which allow the presence of only one dealer, or as open territories, which allow the presence of several dealers. Japanese automobile companies have all opted for open territories.

Having sales companies that belong to the manufacturer's group of affiliated companies *(keiretsu)* and having a territory system are both methods by which Japanese auto companies organize the distribution of their products.

In Toyota's case, the sales affiliates are divided into five groups, each based on a major model line of Toyota cars. (Nissan also has a five-pronged sales affiliate organization.) This kind of arrangement sometimes is called a "multidealer sales organization."

The following are Toyota's five groups of dealers and the product models handled by each group. (Domestic market product names are used here.)

1. Toyota dealerships: Crown, Century, Carina, Soarer
2. Toyopet dealerships: Mark II, Corona, Corsa, Soarer
3. Corolla dealerships: Celica, Camry, Corolla, Corolla II
4. Auto dealerships: Chaser, Sprinter, Starlet
5. Vista dealerships: Cresta, Vista, Tercel

This system maintains almost completely model-specific dealership groups, thereby reducing competition among the groups.

The chief model handled by Toyota dealerships is the top-of-the-line Crown luxury sedan, which is sold primarily to companies.

At Toyopet dealerships, the biggest sellers are the Mark II and Corona models. The Mark II is Toyota's top-of-the-line family car, aimed primarily at individual consumers in the 35- to 45-year age group. The Corona is Toyota's top-of-the-line compact car, aimed at both families and young people.

Corolla dealerships are named after their chief seller, the Corolla. This is also Toyota's biggest seller overall, aimed at families and young people.

Auto dealerships mainly handle the Sprinter, Toyota's highest grade car for the general public.

Vista dealers also are named after their main model, which is a new type of mass-market car seen as the next generation to the Corolla.

Thus, each dealership has its main model, a limited selection of other models, and operates within a well-defined territory. Generally, there is only one dealership for each of the above five groups in each prefecture, although there are two or more in the major metropolitan prefectures. This means that five Toyota dealerships, one from each group, operate in the same territory within what we referred to earlier as an open territory system.

This type of sales organization is particularly beneficial for dealerships that handle the most popular models. On the other hand, it works against the interest of the dealerships that handle the least popular models. It also means that model changes tend to have a big impact on the dealerships. These facts have led Toyota to introduce its *mutual-aid system* whereby dealerships in different groups agree to share certain models. For example, a Toyota dealer that handles mainly Crown passenger models might agree to let the local Toyopet dealer handle all of its Crown commercial models. To reciprocate, the Toyopet allows the Toyota dealer to handle its Corona commercial models. This kind of arrangement offers several advantages:

1. It lessens the impact of a model change (including a minor change) on a specific dealership group by spreading it out among two or more groups. Without the mutual-aid system, dealerships facing a model change would find themselves hard put to sell current

Table 5-2. Toyota's Sales and Service Network

Models handled (Passenger cars)	T Toyota dealers	Tokyo Toyota	Aichi Toyota	Osaka Toyota	Okinawa Toyota	P Toyopet dealers	Tokyo Toyopet	Osaka Toyopet	C Toyota Corolla dealers	Nagoya Toyota Diesel	A Toyota Auto dealers	Toyota Auto Tokyo District	Toyota Auto Osaka District	Toyota Auto Okinawa	V Toyota Vista dealers	Toyota Forklift dealers	Toyota Lease companies
Century	⬤	●	●	●	●		●	●									
Crown	⬤	●	●	◀	●		●	●									
Soarer	⬤	●	●	●	●		●	●									
Supra		●		●		⬤	■			●							
Mark II						⬤	■			●							
Chaser					●				⬤								
Cresta											⬤	●	●	●	●		
Camry									⬤	●		◀		●	●		
Vista										●							
Corona	⬤	●		●	●	⬤					⬤	●	●	●			
Carina		●	●				■	●									
Celica							●		⬤	●							
Corolla									⬤	●							
Sprinter							●		⬤								
Corsa				●		⬤				●					●		
Corolla II																	
Tercel														●			
Starlet											⬤	●	●	●			

Toyota Lease companies: Handles all Toyota models

											Handles all Toyota models
Toyota MR2	●	•	•						●	●	
Sprinter Carib		•	•						●	●	
Dyna	●	•	•	•							
Toyoace		•	•				•	•			
Hiace		•	•	●	●		•	•			
Master Ace	●	•	•	•			•	•			
Town Ace					●	•					
Liteace	●	•	•	•					●	•	•
Hilux	●	•	•	•	•		•	•	•	•	•
Publica Pick-up		•	•						●	•	•
Land Cruiser	●	•	•	•		•					
Blizzard		•	•	•		•				●	
Coaster	●	•	•	•		•					
Industrial vehicles	●			●							●

(Row group label: Trucks)

1. Solid squares indicate dealers that handle only passenger cars and solid triangles dealers that handle only vans.
2. Toyota industrial vehicle dealers include 32 Toyota Forklift dealers. The Toyota dealer handles districts that do not have their own Toyota Forklift dealer (except for the Tokushima District, which is handled by a Toyopet dealer).

[Translator's Note: The above car model names are those used in Japan. Some of these models may use different names in overseas markets.]

models just prior to the introduction of the new model. They would feel pressured to resort to absorption sales and their business results would have bigger fluctuations. By contrast, the mutual-aid system enables the impact of model changes to be spread out. That, plus the fact that each dealership group handles several models, helps spread the sales risks associated with specific models.

2. The mutual-aid system also makes for a more extensive network for parts supply and after-sales service. Again using the previous example of mutual aid in Crown and Corona sales, both dealerships are required to maintain parts supply and after-sales service for both car models. This results in a broader-ranging and stronger after-sales service organization.

Table 5-2 shows the specific relationships between dealership groups and car models handled.

COMPETITION AMONG DEALERSHIP GROUPS

Formally, there is no competition between Toyota dealerships in the same territory, since each belongs to a different group and sells different models aimed at different consumer strata. However, the fact is that the expansion of Toyota's selection of models has caused overlapping among targeted consumer strata. This in turn has led to increasingly severe competition among Toyota dealerships belonging to different groups in the same territory. In other words, the dealership groups are not as distinctive from each other as they used to be.

Let us take as an example the Kanagawa Toyota dealership, which was established in October 1946. This was Toyota's first dealership in Kanagawa Prefecture following the war. Noting the principle that one cup can only hold one cup's worth of

water, Toyota's Kamiya decided to set up a second sales channel for Toyota cars in the region by establishing the first
Toyopet dealership in the region's main city of Yokohama in
January 1956. Later, the Kanagawa Toyota and Yokohama
Toyopet dealerships jointly invested their own capital to establish a Corolla dealership for the region in 1961, then an Auto
dealership in 1968, and finally a Vista dealership in 1979. Over
the years, the competition among these Toyota dealerships in
the same territory has steadily increased.

Obviously, competition among dealerships in the same territories is a positive factor for Toyota's overall sales and is a key
factor behind the strength of the Toyota sales organization.

ADVANTAGES OF USING LOCAL CAPITAL

Of the 314 sales companies (and 4,333 sales outlets) in the
Toyota group, Toyota directly owns (by direct equity investment) only thirteen companies. The other 301 sales companies
(about 96 percent of the total) were established using local
capital. The thirteen wholly owned sales companies consist of
six Tokyo-based companies (including Tokyo Toyota, Tokyo
Toyopet, and Tokyo Corolla), one company based in Osaka
(Osaka Toyopet), five in Sapporo, and one in Fukuoka.

By contrast, nationally, Japan's automakers held full ownership of 20 percent of their sales companies on average,
majority ownership (ranging from 50 to 99 percent of sales
company equity) in another 11 percent, and minority ownership (less than 50 percent of sales company equity) in another
19 percent. The industry average thus shows that exclusively
local capitalization is the case at half of Japan's auto sales
companies. By and large, these locally capitalized sales companies are invested in by prominent local companies.

When we subtract Toyota, who owns only one-tenth of its
sales companies, from the industry average, we see that the

remaining Japanese automakers own on average over 60 percent of their sales companies. The only other automaker whose ownership level is anywhere near as low as Toyota's is the relatively small-scaled competitor, Honda.

Toyota's emphasis on having local business interests capitalize its regional sales companies was part of the sales expansion policy developed early on by Kamiya. This policy reaped the following advantages.

The local managers running these regional sales companies are more serious about succeeding when they know that local business interests have their money invested in these sales companies.

Local ownership also makes it easier for profits to be reinvested in the sales companies that earn them. After all, most managers at sales companies that are fully owned by the parent automaker are employees on loan from the parent company. They tend to think profits should be channeled back to the parent company. Also, they tend to be less concerned with the regional sales company's long-term interests.

The sales power of locally owned regional sales companies is boosted by double support — support from the parent company and support from local investors and the local people who make up almost all of the sales company management.

In addition, the fact that these regional sales companies are owned and operated almost entirely by local people makes it easier to increase sales through social and family ties in the community.

ADVANTAGES OF WHOLLY OWNED DEALERSHIPS

As mentioned earlier, Toyota has thirteen wholly owned dealerships. Most of these are in the two largest metropolitan prefectures of Tokyo and Osaka, where competition among dealerships is the greatest.

All of these wholly owned dealerships were established by the Toyota Motor Sales Company, the formerly separate sales company that has since merged with Toyota Motor. These dealerships were established to secure a solid position in Japan's major urban markets. This strategy stood in stark contrast to the common strategy among rival automakers in the early postwar period of linking up with a foreign-owned company to facilitate the importation of technology for improving production and sales. As such, Toyota's plan posed a direct challenge to dealerships allied with its chief rival , Nissan.

On the other hand, the presence of the Toyota-owned dealerships provided a healthy stimulus to locally owned dealerships. For example, one might think that the goal at the Yokohama Toyopet dealership is to replace the rival Nissan dealership as Number 1 in Kanagawa Prefecture. But they have already achieved that goal. Now, their goal is to become number one in sales results among all Toyopet dealerships, and to do that they must outsell the Toyota-owned Tokyo Toyopet dealership.

Thus, by being the first to carry out strategic investment in certain sales channels, Toyota has achieved the highest level of sales competitiveness among Japan's automakers.

Toyota began taking the lead in this respect in the late 1940s, when it established its strategy of rapidly building up sales strength via the efforts of locally owned dealer/distributors, sales channels, and sales outlets. It goes without saying that the sales network is the nucleus of any company's sales strength. We should also affirm, however, that a good sales network is essential for obtaining good information and communication and for providing extensive after-sales service. Toyota did just these things and thereby reached a prominent position during its formative years.

CHAPTER 6

New Product Development System

FOR ANY automobile manufacturer, car production and sales involves a large and lengthy process. At Toyota, this process can be broken down into three stages: (1) new product research and development (R&D), (2) manufacturing, and (3) sales. Specifically, this first stage of new product R&D consists of conceptual research and development and concrete new product development, the latter of which usually is done in-house. In contrast, the manufacture of parts, an activity within the manufacturing stage, is done usually by outside suppliers. Primarily, Toyota's in-house manufacturing work consists of pressing out car bodies and assembling finished products. The work at the sales stage is handled by Toyota's affiliated sales companies. Any automaker's overall management system must cover the entire group of companies involved in this long process.

Chapter 6 describes Toyota's new product development system, which is part of the first stage, new product R&D. This description is based on three new model development case studies for the car models known in Japan as the Toyota Celica, the Carina ED, and the Corona EXIV. The material used in this chapter comes primarily from two sources: first, an article by Takehiko Morozumi entitled "The Development Story of the New Line of Toyota Celica Cars" *(Nyu Moderu ga Dekiru made: Serika Keiretsu no Baai)* that appeared in the January 1990 issue of *Motor Fan (Motoru Fuan)*; and second, interviews with members of Toyota's product planning division.

OVERVIEW OF TOYOTA'S NEW PRODUCT DEVELOPMENT SYSTEM

At Toyota, new product development falls into three categories: new car models, full model changes, and minor model changes. Rarely does the company come out with a brand new car model, so the great majority of new product development work falls in the two model-change categories. In principle, full model changes follow a four-year cycle and minor model changes a two-year cycle. Each new model is estimated to have a market life of four years. Consequently, once a new model reaches full production and sales, developers begin the conceptual planning work for its successor. The process that begins at this stage and ends with full-scale production takes four years, the same length as the product's estimated market life.

If we include the time required for the basic research that goes into the new car model, product development and initial production stages end up going way beyond the model's market life. Toyota carries out a wide range of basic research at its main R&D center in Toyoda City. More specialized and concrete new-model research is done at other R&D centers, such as the Higashi-Fuji Center and the Parts Center.

The following lists the organizational structure and main activities of the Higashi- Fuji R&D Center.

• *Development Section #11:* Initial development of body, chassis, and drive system.

For example, people in this section perform early design and development of new body structures and steering systems.

• *Development Section #12:* Initial engine development for Engine Sections #1 and #2 of the Design Division.

For example, this section works on reducing exhaust emissions and developing super chargers and engines for motor shows.

• *Research Section #11:* Research on fuel control technologies, alternative fuels, and engine development (prior to the engine development work done by Development Section #12).

For example, this section works on gas turbine engines, methanol engines, fuel analysis, and so on.

• *Research Section #12:* Research on materials (both structural and functional). Also, R&D in electric automobiles and automotive communications technologies.

For example, this section studies ceramic materials, PZT, new types of batteries, and the like.

In addition, the R&D division at Toyota's head office includes the following sections:

• *Material Technology Section:* Development of automotive materials.

For example, they develop new varieties of chrome, resins, rubber, urethane, leather, plastics, superconductors, and composite materials.

• *Microelectronics Development Section:* Development of automotive electronic components (semiconductors, etc.).

For example, they develop ICs and other electronic components.

There is a chief engineer for each car model. This person is the core member of the new product planning team within the Product Planning Division and receives initial technological developments made by the various R&D centers and the head-office R&D division as well as market information gathered by the Merchandise Planning and Sales Divisions.

This transfer of technology and information occurs about three years before the new model reaches its final form.

While the more specific product development work after this point is handled primarily by the head office's Engineering Division, the outside suppliers participate in their respective areas (such as car body suppliers taking part in the model's body development and parts suppliers in the development of various parts).

Figures 6-1A and 6-1B outline Toyota's new product development organization and shows how the new product development process is divided up among the organization's various divisions and sections. The encircled numbers 1 to 10 in Figure 6-1A approximate the temporal sequence of development steps within this organization.

As already mentioned, Japanese automakers generally produce new models on a four-year cycle. However, most European automakers work on a much longer cycle. Mercedes-Benz, for example, has a new model cycle of seven to nine years. According to automotive journalist Takehiko Morozumi, the Japanese build cars from a commercial total quality control (TQC) perspective while Europeans build them from a philosophical perspective. In other words, before getting into the nitty-gritty of technology, the Europeans undertake extensive research on factors such as humankind's relationship with cars, present and future road systems, and the outlook for distribution.

The purpose of undertaking basic scientific research and extensive research into the philosophical question of how cars fit into society is to study how well automobiles serve as a vehicle toward human happiness. This is the focal point from which all new car development should begin.

Figure 6-2 provides a flowchart that counts backward from full-scale production to show approximately how many months before that point each stage of the product develop-

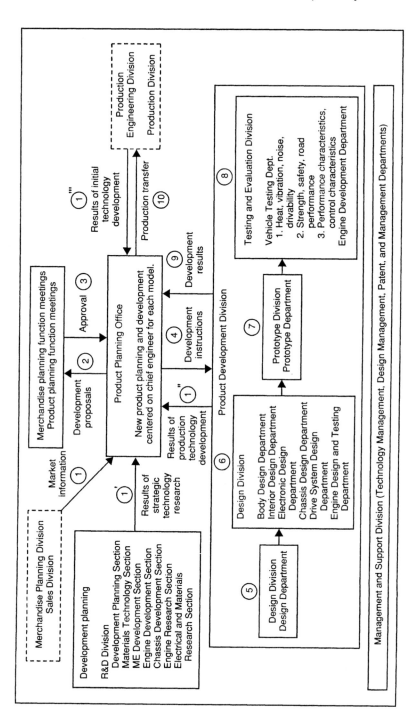

Figure 6-1A. New Product Development Organization

Division/Department/Section		Main tasks	Themes and products
Head office	Development Planning Section	▲ R&D planning and promotion	R&D themes: materials, electronics, engines, chassis, drive systems, resin body parts, air conditioning, vehicle characteristics, communications, safety, welded body parts, electric cars, batteries, etc.
	Product Planning Center	▲ New product planning ▲ Liaison and coordination with other departments as needed for new product development	Products: full or minor model changes for Crowns, Corollas, and development of completely new models such as the MR2.
	Technology Management Division	▲ Management of Engineering Division's organization, equipment, costs, and technical data (reports, etc.) ▲ Cost planning and estimation	Computer processing, CAD, LA, etc.
	Region-specific testing grounds	▲ Evaluation of characteristics in cars for cold-weather regions ▲ Evaluation of high-speed road performance conditions	Starting performance, drivability
	Design Management Division	▲ Management and design support for technical data (diagrams, CAD data, standards, etc.) ▲ Certification processing	Legal processing required for certification and sales
	Patent Department	▲ Acquisition and management of industrial property rights (patent claims, utility model rights, design rights, trademark rights)	
	Design Department	▲ New product style design development	Style design: exterior and interior design, color design, clay model design, style CAD
	Body Design Department	▲ Body design	Body design includes the main body, exterior parts, lamps, mirrors, exhaust pipes, wipers, etc.
	Interior Design Department	▲ Design of interior parts	Interior design includes the instrument panel, interior door handles, seats, seat belts, air conditioning, etc.
	No. 1 Engine Section	▲ Design and testing of commercial-model engines	Development of engines for next production cycle
	No. 2 Engine Section	▲ Design and testing of passenger-model engines	Development of EFI system, carburetors, turbo chargers, etc.

	Department/Section	Function	Details
Head office	Electronic Engineering Department	▲ Design and testing of various electronic control systems	EFI systems, cruise control, battery, TEMS, pneumatic suspension, ABS, navigation, displays, audio, wire harness, etc.
	Chassis Design Department	▲ Chassis parts design	Suspension, steering, brakes, exhaust pipes, fuel system, etc.
	Drive Train Department	▲ Design and testing of drive train systems and parts	Transmissions, differential gears, 4WD, etc.
	Product Testing Department	▲ Comprehensive testing and evaluation of vehicle characteristics	
	No. 1 Vehicle Testing Section	▲ Vehicle testing (heat, vibration, noise, drivability)	Evaluation of cooling and air conditioning, vibration and noise, drivability, field of vision, and visual indicators
	No. 2 Vehicle Testing Section	▲ Vehicle testing (strength, safety, road performance)	Evaluation of body, chassis, drive strength, seats, wipers, rubber parts, exhaust pipes, collision testing, and durability testing
	No. 3 Vehicle Testing Section	▲ Vehicle testing (performance characteristics, control characteristics)	Evaluation of operational safety, drivability, etc.
	Prototype Department	▲ Manufacture of prototypes (preparation and management of prototype parts and manufacturing processes such as presses, sheet metal processing, and assembly)	
	Material Technology Department	▲ Development of automotive materials	Development of paints, chroming, resins, rubber, urethane, leather, plastics, superconductor, composites, etc.
	Microelectronics Development Department	▲ Development of electronic components (semiconductors, etc.)	Development of ICs and other electronic components
	Motor Sports Department	▲ Planning, development, and support for motor sports activities	

Figure 6-1B. Engineering Division Organization

ment process takes place. Now we will have a closer look at the product development stages shown in Figure 6-2.

NEW PRODUCT PLANNING PROCESS

Almost all Japanese automobile manufacturers have a section that exercises comprehensive control over the entire new product development process. The people in this section assume overall responsibility for the new product and help coordinate the development process, such as by issuing instructions to the various relevant departments.

At Toyota, this section is called the Product Planning Center. It is here that we find the new model's chief engineer, the person with ultimate responsibility for the new model. The chief engineer establishes the direction of the new model's development and oversees the development process. Consequently, each new model clearly reflects the thinking and approach of its chief engineer. Figure 6-3 shows a matrix chart that plots the relationship between the chief engineer and the people in the various departments related to the new product's development.

While the product managers usually are graduates of the engineering departments, occasionally they rise up the management ranks instead. The product manager who handled the Nissan Cima's development was a nonengineer manager. It is thought that product managers from the management ranks generally are better able to develop new car models that anticipate market trends than are the more technical-minded engineers. The marketability factor is, of course, very important. However, engineers generally show themselves to be better at supervising the design stages while manager-types are usually better at supervising the product promotion stages.

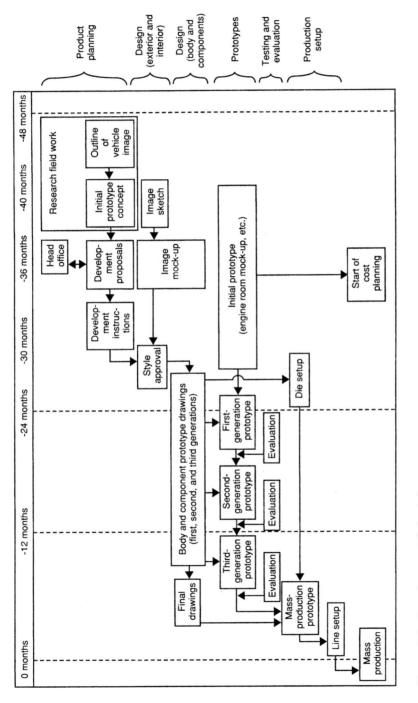

Figure 6-2. Development Schedule

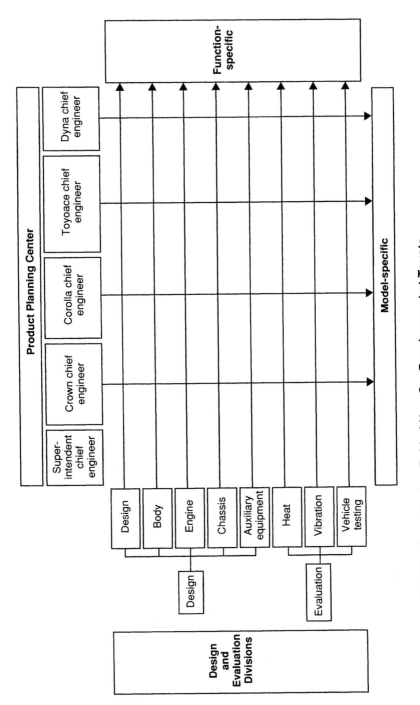

Figure 6-3. The Chief Engineer System Behind New Car Development at Toyota

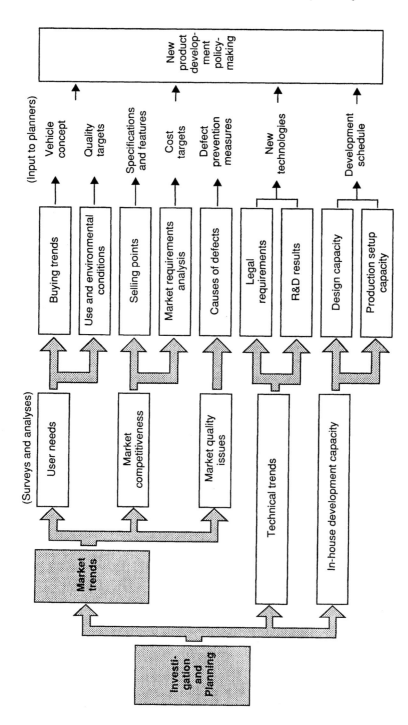

Figure 6-4. New Model Planning Process

Basically, chief engineers take one of the following two approaches to new model development:

1. A *decentralized approach* in which the product planning center plays a pivotal role but the various related departments operate with a relatively large degree of autonomy.
2. A *centralized approach* in which the entire new product development organization is centered on and represented by the project team that is headed by the chief engineer.

The first approach generally works better for the routine work in new product development. The second approach enhances the chief engineers' ability to put their personal stamps on the new product. We will look more closely at the chief engineer's job in a forthcoming section.

As we see in Figure 6-4, the planning process for a new car model is based on a new model image that combines market trends with technical trends. The basic planning process in this figure shows considerations such as user needs, product positioning in the market, and ways to address quality problems in current models form the backbone of the market research. This strict approach is part of the strength of Japanese cars and is undoubtedly one reason for their high quality.

Market research begins with surveys to understand the public's reaction to recently introduced current models. This involves more than simply collecting data. Often, the chief engineer personally interviews domestic dealers or overseas importers to find out firsthand what salespeople and users are saying in various sales regions. In addition, members of the Merchandise Planning Office, who look at the merchandise value of automobiles, interview domestic and overseas dealers and sales managers to get input they can use when planning the next model.

However, considering that all of this market research data concerns only reactions to previous or current products, the new product planners must also try to look four years ahead and anticipate the social environment and trends that could affect product marketability. Product planners know that they can never rely completely on data based solely on current opinions and perceptions. They should place a high value on input from younger people in the company. By introducing its new flat organization, Toyota is doing just that.

NEW CAR STYLING PROCESS

The exterior design process at Toyota uses an initial development team in addition to the line team in the Design Division, which enables the design planning process to get started earlier. Usually, this process begins about forty months before the new car's market debut.

Once the line team has finished preparing minor changes for the most recent new model on the market, it switches over to design work for the next-generation new model. This means that they cannot begin work on the next-generation model until about ten months after the new model has been brought to market.

Design work begins with idea sketches as a method of image development to create a new concept. After that, they begin to make three-dimensional models, such as ceramic models, to study and evaluate the aesthetic features of the car's form.

Next, they draw more sketches to render a more detailed picture of the car design. Often, this step is followed immediately by the creation of a five-to-one scale model. Since there is only so much time available for this design work, designers tend to prefer three-dimensional models over two-dimensional drawings because the 3-D renderings give a better idea of the image. These models are called "mock-ups." It takes from twenty to thirty days to complete each mock-up.

The following step is to make a full-size clay model. This model is submitted for approval as part of the new car's planning proposal. This approval should come within a year after the start of the design work, which leaves about thirty months before the new car hits the market.

The interior design is started later than the exterior design, but it is submitted for approval at about the same time.

Because the design team is given only one year to come up with its new car planning proposal, the question of how much time to allot for initial concept development is critical.

NEW CAR DESIGN PROCESS

The timetable for each model change design is built around the body design work.

Once the new car design proposal ("style") is approved, the designers draw up a line chart for the car body. They use this line chart as a basis for the body sheet metal design. When completed, the body sheet metal design drawings — which are the original drawings for the body structure — are given to the die-cast and press engineers who begin preparing dies for manufacturing the car body.

Toyota and other automakers that manufacture many types of cars and trucks treat component/part design and development as a separate process from new model design. They usually select basic component designs from among the wide variety of designs available and then make detailed design changes to suit the new model design. Nowadays, many design departments use Computer-aided Design/Computer-aided Manufacturing (CAD/CAM) systems. Among other tasks, these systems simplify and accelerate the process of determining the three-dimensional data for basic body designs. Some CAD systems are equipped with style programs that program numerically controlled (NC) machines to make first-draft "clean models." Others can automatically make line drawings based on the dimensional measurements of the final mock-up. There are also some systems that can make design drawings for the detailed body design.

The CAM technology of the CAD/CAM system has been used to design press dies and to make them using CAM-programmed NC machining centers. Almost every Japanese automaker now uses a CAM system for die design and fabrication.

Another popular computer application in car design work is the computer-based simulation system, which is often used in structural analysis. In this instance, the computer simulates the vibration stroke against the suspension to check the suspension's vibration characteristics. These kinds of computer applications fall under the category of Computer-aided Engineering (CAE).

NEW CAR PROTOTYPE PROCESS

The design process runs concurrently with the prototype fabrication and test/evaluation process. This prototype process is needed early on so that the designers can see as soon as possible how their designs actually work and can make corrective changes. The prototype process is a cycle with several steps.

As illustrated in Figure 6-5, the three main steps in the prototype process are the (1) initial prototype, (2) official prototype, and (3) production prototype. The development of each prototype takes place via the following process.

Make and/or buy prototype dies and jigs → Make and/or buy prototype parts → Conduct acceptance inspection of

Initial Prototypes

New car model designs and component designs that feature entirely new functions or use entirely new materials are difficult to evaluate due to a lack of market data and other basic evaluation data. Because of this fact and because it takes a long time to develop a new car model, it helps to have initial prototypes that can be used for practical evaluation at an early stage in the development process.

After 3 or 4 initial prototypes

Official Prototype

Working from the new technologies developed for the initial prototypes, the official prototype represents a commercially viable product. To get to this stage, the official prototype must be tested for reliability, performance, productivity, serviceability, maintainability, and other characteristics.

Production Prototype

At this step, the new car model prototype is sent from the Prototype Department to the Production Setup Department, where the production prototype is made using ordinary production equipment. During this manufacturing work, the production equipment and processes used to make the prototype are evaluated and the prototype evaluation results are checked against the Prototype Department's prototype evaluation results to make sure they are the same.

Full-scale production

Figure 6-5. Prototype Process Flow

*prototype parts → Send parts to presses → Press parts →
Weld on sheet metal parts → Assemble body shell → Paint
body shell → Assemble prototype vehicle → Inspect finished
prototype vehicle*

Naturally, a schedule must be made for all of the production processes required for this sequence of steps.

Almost all of the body welding work is done manually. After the body panels have been pressed, veteran welders perform the finish welding ("brazing") along with some spot welding. Recently, CAD/CAM systems and sophisticated industrial robots have taken over some of this work.

At the initial prototype step, the new car model's unit components are manufactured and tested even before the car's style has been finalized. In many cases, the people who make initial prototypes simply remodel unit components from current car models to make them resemble the new-model design.

Also at this step, the engine room produces a full-size engine mock-up as realistically as possible and studies the layout and assembly logistics of the various unit components in the engine. Sometimes, the new car model is scheduled to offer a wide selection of engines and transmission types, and in such cases several mock-ups must be made at the initial prototype step.

The official prototype step includes three generations of prototypes. The prototype testing process at this step involves checking characteristics ranging from reliability and performance to productivity, serviceability, and maintainability. Reports on problems identified during this testing are fed back to the designers who must then come up with corrective improvements.

The processing of manufacturing and testing three generations of official prototypes easily can involve the manufacture of more than 300 prototype cars. The production cost for each prototype, exclusive of labor costs, comes to several hundred thousand dollars, and even more for luxury models. Consequently, Toyota and other car makers must budget nearly $8 million for the prototype process for each new car model.

Toyota carries out four or five model changes per year, which means its prototype factories turn out more than 1,000 prototypes in a year. When the final, third-generation official prototype has been produced, the prototype work shifts to the production prototype step. Here, too, there are at least two generations of prototypes, and various detailed checks are made on each prototype.

NEW CAR TESTING AND EVALUATION PROCESS

This is the most time- and labor-consuming part of the new car development process. The people involved in new car development estimate that about half of all the energy they spend to develop a new car is spent in the new car testing and evaluation process.

The multitude of test categories include dynamic characteristics, ride comfort, drivability, and safety. All together, there are some 200 kinds of tests and 3,200 specific test items. Because each new car model has thousands of possible component combinations, the evaluation standards must differ from one combination to the next to account for each combination's different characteristics that require evaluation.

To help rationalize the complex testing schedule, most automakers have established a Computer-aided Testing (CAT) system. The tests are broadly divided into two groups:

1. *Tests to confirm basic functions and reliability.*

    The contents and evaluation criteria for these tests have been standardized to a large degree, so that much of these tests have become routine work. Usually, the results are fed back to the designers. Some of these tests have been moved back to earlier development stages, such as the initial prototype step or steps where CAE systems are used.

As mentioned earlier, there are thousands of test items, and these are carried out thoroughly to check the quality of each part. Typical of the best Japanese manufacturing, these tests are based on the user's perspective and are designed to take into account every imaginable user need.

2. *Running tests to check for road performance characteristics.*

These tests, which include indoor tests, test-course performance tests, and road tests on actual public roads, are designed to evaluate the car's overall performance characteristics and its "feel" for the driver and passengers.

TOYOTA'S CHIEF ENGINEER SYSTEM

As mentioned earlier, a chief engineer is assigned to each new Toyota car under development as the person most responsible for that development project. In other words, the chief engineer is the chief developer. Let us now take a closer look at Toyota's chief engineer system. (Much of the material in this section is borrowed from Shigeru Shiozawa's book *Toyota Motor's Development Chief System* [Toyota Jidosha Kaihatsu Shusa Seido], published by Kodansha in 1987.)

It has long been thought that sales is Toyota's greatest strength. Just after World War II, Toyota's Shōtarō Kamiya successfully led an ambitious campaign to build a comprehensive nationwide sales network. Without a doubt, a company's sales strength is derived largely from the numbers of its sales outlets and sales staff. This was definitely the case at Toyota.

However, no matter what the product is, it takes more than a sales organization to make it sell — the product must also have sales appeal. In Japan, Nissan's Cima model of luxury cars and Asahi's "super-dry" beer are two recent examples of hot-selling products whose success has been based primarily upon product sales strength. In other words, if a company can develop a product that responds to user needs with perfect accuracy, it will be a big seller. Product strength, or marketability, therefore remains a key factor in product development.

How, then, does the chief engineer system operate at Toyota for the development of new car models?

Toyota's Product Planning Office occupies the fifth and sixth floors (about 300 square meters) of Engineering Building No. 6 at the company's head office in Toyoda City.

On the fifth floor, there are eleven chief engineer teams for passenger cars (private vehicles); on the sixth floor, there are almost twenty chief engineer teams for commercial vehicles (including wagons, vans, trucks, and buses). Each team has its own group of desks.

The members on each chief engineer team for passenger cars number between ten and fifteen. Most of them are of middle-management rank such as section chief or chief clerk, who do not work directly on the line but have specialist management duties.

The Product Planning Center is a relatively small division staffed by about 500 people, including managers. However, four of these people are of executive-director rank. This attests to the decidedly strong emphasis Toyota places upon new car development. It can even be said that the Production Planning Office is the nucleus of the entire company.

What is the role of the chief engineer team members? Let us suppose that, for example, a member of a particular chief engineer's team is someone on loan from one of the design offices in the Design Division. His or her responsibilities naturally would include communicating the chief engineer's intentions to the design offices, listening to their reactions, and reporting back to the chief engineer. Thus, based on background, this individual becomes the chief engineer's design liaison agent.

Likewise, team members that come from other divisions function as liaison agents with their "home" divisions, facilitating two-way communication regarding new designs for engines, car bodies, interior components, and so on.

How does someone rise up through the ranks at Toyota to become a chief engineer? Let us consider a few typical examples. After graduating from a technical university (in the machinery department), Employee A joins Toyota and spends his first eight years there working in the Design Division. While in the Design Department, he participated in the design of Corolla and Corolla II models. Next, he was assigned to the Product Planning Office to be a member of the chief engineer teams for new models in the Celica and Carina lines. Finally, he was promoted to chief engineer for the next new Celica model.

Here is another example: Employee B graduated from the industrial design department at an industrial arts university and joined Toyota to put his specialty (design of mass-produced industrial products) to work. Naturally, he was also assigned to Toyota's Design Division. Later, he was promoted to the Product Planning Office, where he was a member of the chief engineer teams (an assistant chief engineer, in fact) for new models of the Corona and the Mark II. Finally, he was promoted to chief engineer for new models in the Soarer line and other lines.

A third and final example: This person graduated from the machinery department at a technical university, then joined Toyota, where he first worked in the Vibration Testing Department. After a stint there, as well as in the departments that test and evaluate chassis and handling characteristics, he was assigned to an R&D team and later to the Chassis Design Section to help design the chassis for a new Crown model. Next, he was promoted to the Product Planning Office, where he was a member of the chief engineer teams for new models of the Celica and Carina. After a time in the Product Technology Development Section, he was returned to the Product Planning Office and was made chief engineer for the fifth-generation Corolla, and later for the sixth-generation Corolla.

All three of these examples are typical of the process by which Toyota employees become chief engineers. Generally, they begin either as line-based designers or employees in the Design Division. In either instance they acquire experience by helping to develop new car models. Next, they join the Product Planning Office and serve as chief engineer team members for certain models. Finally, they are promoted to the position of chief engineer.

Incidentally, we might note that Toyota currently has twenty passenger car lines, each of which includes thousands of variations. The Corolla, for example, includes the following eight body types:

1. sedan four-door 1,500-cc GL Saloon
2. sedan five-door 1,660-cc ZX
3. three-door 1,600-cc FX-GT
4. five-door 1,500-cc FX-G
5. levin three-door GTV
6. levin two-door GT
7. wagon 1,800-cc diesel GL
8. four-door van 1,800-cc diesel GL

As a result, each car line competes for the same users, establishing a strong rivalry among the chief engineers of each car line.

There are other matters of interpersonal relations that come into play in the Design Planning Office. For example, if a chief engineer selects a certain newly designed part to use in his or her car but another chief engineer has already ordered the same part design, the latecomer must get permission from the earlier chief engineer before using the part.

Although all eleven passenger-car chief engineers have their desks on the same floor, there is still a keen sense of rivalry among them. Each works with a strong sense of independence. By contrast, there is little discord between chief engineers and their team members, who work very closely for the duration of the development project.

Since there are only eleven passenger-car chief engineers for twenty passenger car models, all but one of the chief engineers is responsible for at least two passenger car models. For example, the chief engineer for the Corolla, which alone accounts for about a quarter of Toyota's total sales, is also the chief engineer for the Sprinter and for the Nova cars produced in America by NUMMI, a Toyota-GM joint venture company.

Toyota adopted this chief engineer system back in 1953, when the growing variety of Toyota models made it no longer feasible for Toyota's president to assume direct responsibility for each new model's development.

THE CHIEF ENGINEER'S ROLE IN THE MATRIX ORGANIZATION

In the previous section, we examined the chief engineer system at Toyota, in which a matrix organization mixes model-specific chief engineers with representatives from various company divisions such as design and testing and evaluation. In this matrix, the division representatives are the horizontal threads in the matrix and stand for line-based work; the chief engineers make up the vertical threads as independent product developers.

The chief engineer for each new car model is just one person and must be able to direct the thorough implementation of the development plan and assume the ultimate authority and responsibility for the overall product development process and its results.

As was shown in the matrix diagram, chief engineers are not line-based workers but management staff workers. Therefore, their authority is not limited to a particular part of the company. Their daily work mainly involves going from department to department to instruct and persuade people. Chief engineers have the authority to issue "development manuals" for their new car models to all relevant company divisions. However, there is no guarantee that the staff in those divisions will carry out the chief engineers' instructions to the letter.

For example, let us suppose a chief engineer issues instructions for a certain type of body design. If he or she gets firm opposition from the team member who represents the body design department (and is consequently ranked at about section-chief level), the idea must be dropped. Even though the chief engineer clearly outranks the opposing team member, the latter has the right to oppose the chief engineer's proposals. Therefore, it is very important that the chief engineer be able to persuade the team members of the value of his or her proposals. The team members are like the arms and legs of chief engineers — they must coordinate them and work closely with them to get anything done. This can be a difficult job, indeed.

Fortunately, chief engineers work directly with their team members, which facilitates this kind of persuasion. However, it is not always easy for the team members to get the instructions carried out by the divisions they represent, whether it be the design division, engine division, or whatever. In each division, corresponding team members have a series of managers

— supervisors, section chiefs, chief clerks, and so on down the management line — that they must persuade, and everyone's cooperation is needed to make the details of the development project happen.

Over the many years of the chief engineer system, Toyota has developed a smoothly functioning system in which the chief engineers enjoy very strong authority and influence in accordance with the "ten-point code of ethics for chief engineers" that will be described next. As a result, it rarely happens that instructions passed down from the chief engineer's team are not carried out as intended.

In a sense, chief engineers are like orchestra conductors. They alone have the baton and alone are ultimately responsible for the harmony of the music. They help to create the music by communicating their intentions to the orchestra members. Therefore, they must be more than managers — they also must inspire those whom they direct with their ideas and strong convictions. This type of inspiration runs throughout the orchestra or, in Toyota's case, throughout the company. Chief engineers must not only be conductors but also philosophers.

Recognizing that it takes a person of exceptional qualities to successfully fill the important post of chief engineer, Toyota promotes a code of ethics for chief engineers. It was written and handed down by Tatsuo Hasegawa, chief engineer of both the first and second generations of Toyota's biggest seller, the Corolla. Toyota's "Ten-point Code of Ethics for Engineers" states the following:

1. Chief engineers must cultivate wide knowledge and keen insight.
2. Chief engineers must possess a personal strategy and plan.
3. Chief engineers must spread a wide and beneficial web of influence.

4. Chief engineers must apply their knowledge and abilities to attain good results.
5. Chief engineers must not begrudge repetitive work.
6. Chief engineers must possess self-confidence.
7. Chief engineers must never pass the buck.
8. Chief engineers and their team members must all be of good character. Any criticism within the team should be made as self-criticism.
9. Chief engineers must make themselves well understood.
10. Chief engineers must possess the following qualities:
    - knowledge and skill
    - perceptiveness, keen judgment, and decisiveness
    - ability to see the large-scale picture
    - lack of emotionalism and a quiet, calm attitude
    - energy and persistence
    - concentration
    - leadership ability
    - expressiveness and persuasiveness
    - flexibility
    - selflessness (unselfishness).

Let us examine some of the more important of the ten points in the code of ethics.

Point 5, not begrudging repetitive work, has to do with the injunction that chief engineers should reflect each day on their day's thoughts and actions. They should not hesitate to emphasize repeatedly important matters when working with higher-ups or co-workers.

This relates to Point 6, which is to have self-confidence. While this does not mean self-confidence to the point of obstinacy, it does mean overcoming any sense of ambivalence about one's abilities. People who are self-confident can calmly devise good plans even under stressful circumstances. (This self-confidence should be tempered with the flexibility mentioned in Point 10.) The combination of self-confidence and flexibility is what we sometimes call "tact" — chief engineers should sense when it is necessary to make compromises and propose face-saving alternatives.

In sum, the purpose of the code of ethics is to help cultivate people who have both a broad perspective and a discerning, decisive sense of authority and leadership.

It might pay to ask why the post of chief engineer is a general management post (staff position) not directly attached to a line of authority in any particular division. The reason is that if chief engineers were at the direct top of a division, their instructions would have to be followed as direct orders. The managers and workers in the division would not work with as much energy or enthusiasm if they were simply following orders. No one at Toyota is too highly ranked to ignore the importance of major model changes when each model change incurs total development costs of more than $230 million. Model changes, although devised by chief engineers, do not get off to a real start until the chief engineers have convinced top management of their worth. If an initial presentation to top managers meets with objections, the chief engineer must come up with materials to persuade the objectors to change their minds.

THE CHIEF ENGINEER'S PHILOSOPHY

What kind of concepts and philosophy do chief engineers embrace as a basis for gaining support from others?

This relates to the question of what kind of car will be in demand by society over the next few years. It takes four years to develop a new car model, and the market life of each new model is also four years. Therefore, from the initial planning stage, designers must look eight years forward in considering such marketing factors as social environment, economic conditions, industrial structure, consumer groups, life-styles, trends among competitors, and technological trends. In short, planners must attempt to predict what the market mainstream will appear like several years in the future.

Already, consumers in Japan have everything that would be considered a necessity. This has created a new era of greater discretion among consumers, who can choose from among various luxury products as well as necessities. Young people no longer simply try to accumulate fancy products. Instead, they are aiming toward a new kind of affluence in which the products they buy are expressions of their life-style. When they shop for a car, they evaluate the models they see not only in terms of price and functions but also in terms of their image as "urban" or "high-tech" and so on. In other words, they want to buy a car that fits in with what they perceive as their life-style and personal values. This point was emphasized by Mr. Fumio Agetsuma, who was the chief engineer of the fourth-generation Corolla. When designing this Corolla, he came up with five key points for ensuring a successful model change:

1. Attractive design.
2. Economy, not just in terms of low fuel consumption but also in terms of high durability and reliability, and superb serviceability. (The latter factors add up to lower maintenance costs.)
3. Riding comfort for driver and passengers.
4. The introduction of new technologies and mechanisms. Model changes have no impact if they use the same engine as the previous model.
5. Competitive pricing.

More recently, of the three key elements in any passenger-car "hit" product, namely style, engine, and suspension, style has come to the forefront as the most important element. Whether it be in a catalog or on a television commercial, the consumer's first impression of the car is always its style. A car whose style turns off buyers will not sell, no matter how excellent the engine and suspension might be. Conversely, if the car's style is attractive, that alone will bring prospective buyers into the dealerships, where they can begin looking at other features, such as the engine and suspension.

Does the chief engineer's philosophy become incorporated directly and wholly into the new model he or she is in charge of developing? In determining the most important element — the car's styling — and especially the car exterior design as described earlier, the chief engineer must work with other managers in the relevant departments in the manner to be described.

First, the chief engineer presents his or her ideas. Explaining the car exterior design ideas to the design managers may involve several rounds of discussions, during which everyone arrives at an understanding concerning not only the design dimensions but also the mood of the design. They draw image sketches to illustrate these ideas. Next, a 5-to-1 scale model is built and shown to sales managers. After that, a full-scale model is built. This model is then presented at a new car development meeting, where designers and sales managers can offer their opinions. These meetings are attended by top managers, such as the chairman or president, and usually produce some improvements to determine the final style.

While the chief engineer's ideas are the foundation, the final style also incorporates input, or suggested improvements, of other people from various departments. Therefore, the decision-making process that produces the final car design is a consensus-building process. This process of decision-making by consensus has been pointed out as a disadvantage by some critics who argue that it tends to produce cars that lack flair and distinctiveness due to the lack of individuality in the design process.

CHAPTER 7

Production Management System: Integration of SIS, CIM, and JIT

ADVANCES IN computer-based data communications technologies have enabled manufacturing companies to build in-house information networks and to set up data communications linkages with sales companies, parts contractors, and material suppliers.

SIS, CIM, AND JIT

Strategic Information System (SIS) utilizes the word "strategic" because the very existence of such an information system has strategic significance. It is *not* an information system that serves the company by distributing "strategic information."

When an entire group of companies is linked by an information network such as an SIS, with each sales company, final products manufacturer, and supplier interconnected as members of an integrated network, information on current market needs can reach the right people very quickly.

In other words, information concerning demand changes in the marketplace (such as changes in consumer preferences and sales trends for certain product types and quantities) can be passed swiftly along to the people in product development, sales, production, and parts procurement, who in turn can respond more quickly. This adds up to a more responsive company or corporate group.

At Toyota, much labor has gone into the development of a strategic information system called the Toyota Network System (TNS). Within TNS, Toyota has an in-house production information system called Assembly Line Control (ALC). ALC includes information used in Computer-aided Manufacturing (CAM) and Computer-aided Planning (CAP) systems, both of which fall under the general category of Computer-integrated Manufacturing (CIM). Another element in CIM is Computer-aided Design (CAD). We discussed CAD in Chapter 6 and will not study it again here.

To enable practical application of SIS and CIM at the factory level, Toyota has developed a production management infrastructure that is referred to as the Toyota production system or the just-in-time (JIT) production system. Its main elements include the *kanban* system, production leveling, and improvement activities.

This chapter briefly describes how production managers at Toyota have utilized SIS, CIM, and JIT in their production management organization.

TOYOTA'S STRATEGIC INFORMATION SYSTEM

A SIS or CIM must include more than a computer-based communications network. One key element in the Toyota Group's SIS is the *order entry system* by which sales companies (dealers, etc.) pass along orders and other sales data to the parent company (Toyota Motors).

Another key element is the mechanism for converting the sales data received by Toyota into instructions for production scheduling. This conversion of data to production orders must be done not only for Toyota's own production operations but also for those of Toyota's many parts suppli-

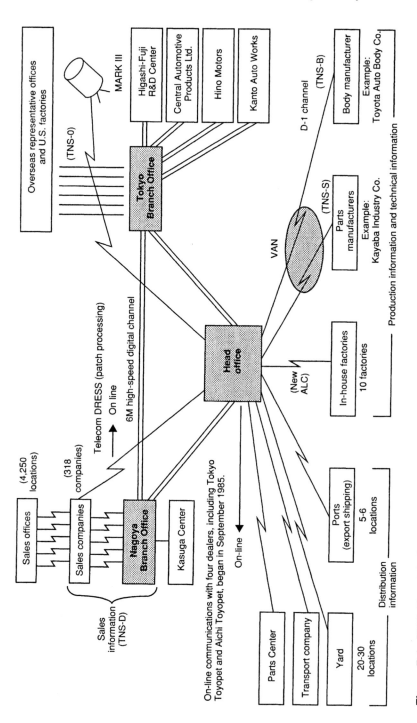

Figure 7-1. TNS: Toyota's Strategic Information System

ers. Figure 7-1 illustrates Toyota's TNS, its strategic information system.

The TNS shown in Figure 7-1 includes the following six subsystems:

1. TNS-D: a network linking Toyota with its dealers
2. TNS-B: a network linking Toyota with its body manufacturers
3. TNS-S: a network linking Toyota with its suppliers
4. New ALC system: New automobile production order system (for Toyota's in-house production)
5. Sales office information system
6. TNS-O: a network linking Toyota with its overseas assembly plants and representative offices

TNS-D: ORDER ENTRY SYSTEM BETWEEN TOYOTA AND TOYOTA DEALERS

Toyota uses information from its dealers when planning production schedules. There are two main steps in this process. Step 1 determines the estimated production schedule for the following month. (This is mainly the master production schedule for finished products and the parts delivery table.) Step 2 determines daily production orders for implementing the daily production schedule. (This consists primarily of setting up a delivery timetable for finished products and an assembly line feed-in sequence of parts for various product models.)

Let us examine these two steps more closely.

STEP 1: DETERMINE THE MONTHLY PRODUCTION SCHEDULE (MASTER PRODUCTION SCHEDULE AND PARTS DELIVERY TABLE)

This step starts with sales plans sent from the sales divisions. These plans relate to both domestic and overseas sales divisions.

Toyota dealers in Japan send the domestic sales division a monthly report forecasting demand for each product line over the next three months. These demand forecast figures are tallied up under product-line categories and major specification categories. Also monthly, the overseas sales division receives overseas orders for the next three months. These figures also are categorized in some detail concerning product specifications.

The production planning division coordinates these two sources of demand information into a single production plan for the next three months. The total volume of finished products (automobiles) to be produced during the first month is divided into daily output figures for each product line. This division is oriented toward *production leveling*, allowing an even work load during all regular working days. The resulting schedule is called the *master production schedule*.

The major specification categories include various combinations of body type, engine type (classified by piston displacement, fuel consumption, etc.), transmission type (gear shift method, etc.), and product grade (luxury car, etc.).

Next, a bill of materials is made up based on the master production schedule to establish a materials requirement plan (MRP). Whether they call it MRP or something else, all automakers have some plan by which they estimate the required parts and materials.

Once it has the data on required materials and parts, Toyota notifies its own assembly plants and its affiliated suppliers of its needs. These notices are called *parts delivery tables*.

However, as we will examine in more detail later on, the parts and materials suppliers are not expected to follow the parts delivery table to the letter. Instead, their daily production volumes are determined primarily by the more detailed and up-to-date instructions that circulate under the kanban system.

STEP 2: DETERMINE THE DAILY PRODUCTION SCHEDULE (FEED-IN SEQUENCE)

At this step, the production planners must figure out exactly how many cars to produce in each model and specification category. The final assembly feed-in sequence is determined as follows, based on ten-day and single-day orders received from dealers. We will examine each of these steps.

Step 1: Dealers send in their ten-day orders to the Toyota sales division office in Nagoya.

Step 2: The Toyota sales division also receives daily orders (also called daily revisions) from dealers.

Step 3: The sales division sends the daily order information to the manufacturing division.

Step 4: The detailed data concerning daily feed-in schedules are sent to the relevant Toyota assembly plants and affiliated suppliers.

Step 1 involves dealers sending in their ten-day orders to the Toyota sales division. These ten-day orders must remain

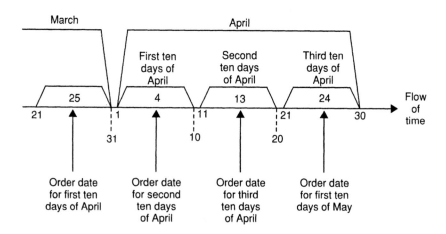

Figure 7-2. Reception of Ten-day Orders from Dealers

within the framework of total monthly volume set by the master production schedule. One week or eight days prior to production, the dealers send the Toyota sales division ten-day orders that indicate the selected options for each final specification category. (See Figure 7-2.) The final specifications combine the major specifications described earlier and the selected options and colors.

The production management divisions uses these ten-day orders to plan daily production volumes for each assembly line and each product line. This represents a revision of the master production plan.

Next, the production planners use the actual customer-specified orders to revise (within a range of plus or minus 10 percent) the production orders derived from the total orders sent to the sales division from dealers across the country. (See

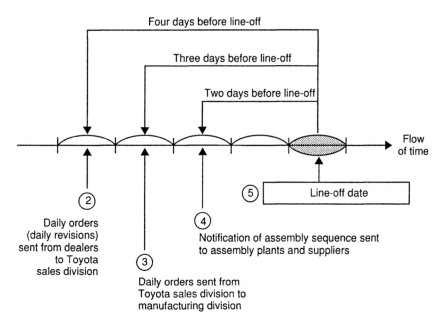

Figure 7-3. Steps from Dealer Orders to Line-off

Figure 7-3.) For example, to accommodate a customer-specified order, they might change the color of a car scheduled for shipment on June 1 from white to red. These *daily revisions* are made four days prior to the date when the finished car is scheduled to roll off the line.

Daily revisions are allowable within the framework of the number of vehicles scheduled for each dealer. Ten-day orders can be revised up to about 23 percent. The average revision is about 10 percent, which is why we used the figure of 10 percent in describing the daily revisions.

Next, the computers in the Toyota sales division sort out the dealer orders according to car model, body type, engine type, grade, transmission type, color, and so on.

Once sorted out, these data are sent to Toyota assembly plants three days before the line-off date for the ordered automobiles. There is no way to overemphasize the importance of these data — they are what tell the Toyota assembly plant managers exactly what they will be required to produce in three days time.

Finally, the manufacturing division uses daily revision data from the sales division to set up a feed-in sequence for the mixed assembly lines. Even without any delays, the assembly plant has only two days before the line-off date to prepare for the feed-in sequence.

Notice that the feed-in sequence schedules are made and issued on a daily basis. Figure 7-3 illustrates the ordering process from Steps 2 to 4. Thanks to this four-step ordering process, there is a period of only four days between the sales division's receipt of the dealer's order and the ordered automobile rolling off the assembly line. The actual manufacturing-line lead time, from the start of the body welding line to the end of the final assembly line, is only one day.

Naturally, the lead time for shipping the ordered cars to the dealers varies according to the distance and transport system between the assembly plant and the dealer.

HOW THE ASSEMBLY LINE USES THE
FEED-IN SEQUENCE DATA

On the assembly line, the only thing the line workers need to know is the type of automobile to be assembled next. The final assembly line has a computer terminal with a CRT display and printer to receive and display this information.

The data indicating the kind of automobile to assemble next are sent from the central computer, which calculates the data based on the feed-in sequence schedule. These data are sent to the display terminal via an on-line real-time communications link.

In addition to displaying various other information, this display terminal also prints out an adhesive label for each car to be assembled, stating its model and specifications. The assembly line workers read these labels to see exactly what kind of car they are to make. Toyota uses labels and feed-in sequence schedules at its assembly lines only. To control the production volume at almost all other processes from forging to machining and subassembly, Toyota uses the kanban system.

Labels and feed-in sequences are used frequently by suppliers who supply main assembly components to the final assembly line, such as transmissions and engines. This is based on the production concept of the *sequential pull method*. Feed-in sequences are used sometimes at body welding lines and painting lines.

The feed-in sequence for wide-variety, small-lot production of subassembly parts directs the operations of subassembly lines and parts supplier lines. As such, they are coordinated with the feed-in sequence schedules at the Toyota final assembly lines, which "pull" the required subassembled parts through the various upstream lines.

Apart from these lines, all other parts production processes and supplier lines are regulated by the kanban system. In other words, the kanban system functions as a "supply support" system for the sequential pull production system.

DISTRIBUTION-LEVEL ON-LINE SYSTEM

After receiving a customer order, the dealer naturally would like the lead time to delivery to be as short as possible. This includes the time required for processing the order information. To help dealers respond more quickly to customer orders with shorter delivery periods, Toyota has built an on-line communications network to link the company with its dealers and to expedite daily order processing.

This on-line Toyota-dealer network uses the nationwide optical fiber cable route that recently has been put into operation by NTT, Japan's largest telephone company. This route is known as Japan's most extensive high-speed, high-capacity digital trunk route.

The network links central mainframe computers in the Toyota head office in Toyoda City and the branch office in Nagoya with computers and terminals at Toyota dealerships. Every day, the dealers send in their order data, which go immediately into the four-step ordering process described previously to minimize delivery lead time.

This network supports three main types of communication functions: real-time processing, file transfer, and electronic mail. In addition, Toyota has developed its own business protocol to enable linkage between various types of computers. This utilizes a basic element in the standard protocol referred to as open systems interconnection (OSI).

This OSI network has made various kinds of activities possible. First, it enables Toyota to keep close tabs on the product stock data maintained by each dealer. It also enables dealers to meet orders quickly by providing each other with ordered cars that are already in stock at a neighboring dealership. In addition, it allows Toyota to make last-minute changes, such as sending a certain car to Dealer B instead of Dealer A — if Dealer B needs it more urgently.

The network also enables Toyota to inform dealers of the latest trends regarding fast-selling and slow-selling car models and to provide dealers with advice on making orders. This is the same kind of information-sharing that occurs at department stores and supermarkets via POS (point-of-sale) communication systems.

These kinds of communications between Toyota and its dealers are centered in the Nagoya branch office (formerly the head office of the now-defunct Toyota Motor Sales Company).

OVERSEAS INFORMATION NETWORK (TNS-O)

This is the basic communication network linking Toyota in Japan with Toyota America in the United States. These connections are made via ordinary public telephone lines and enable Toyota to stay in direct touch with its assembly plants and offices in various parts of North America. By keeping track of order data, shipping data, and parts distribution data in a timely manner, it helps Toyota provide better service to customers.

INFORMATION SYSTEM BETWEEN TOYOTA AND ITS SUPPLIERS

PARTS DELIVERY TABLE

As the finished product manufacturer, once a month Toyota sends its parts manufacturers an estimate of its production output for the next three months. This notification is made in the form of a *parts delivery table* as shown in Figure 7-4. The parts manufacturers use the contents of this table for the next month to estimate how many parts they will need to deliver each day. The figures for the subsequent two months are looser estimates that are subject to revision in the parts delivery table to be issued next month.

Sometimes, the production output is changed slightly even during the current month. These minor changes are the parts delivery adjustments made under the kanban system.

Under this system, the finished product manufacturers sends out a parts delivery table to each of its parts suppliers. This table specifies (using part numbers) the quantity of each type of part to be delivered. The following shows the total amounts to be delivered of one type of part (Part C, for example) during a three-month period.

The parts delivery table shows the following three-month estimates for Part C:

1. Parts to be delivered during the month of May 199X: 1,600
2. Estimated parts to be delivered during June: 1,600
3. Estimated parts to be delivered during July: 1,700

The total for (1) is a fairly accurate figure that is subject only to minor adjustment under the kanban system. The totals for (2) and (3) are more loosely estimated figures that are subject to change in the next monthly parts delivery table. To save space, Figure 7-4 shows only the information for (1).

The parts delivery table also specifies how many parts are in each case (10, in this example).

The table shows the daily and monthly totals for each type of part to be delivered. Since May in Japan contains several national and company holidays, we can see that zero parts were delivered on May 3, 4, 5, 11, 12, 18, 19, 25, or 26. During the twenty-two workdays in the month of May, the amount delivered has been leveled out to seven cases per day.

Actually, seven cases per day for twenty-two days equals ($7 \times 10 \times 22 =$) 1,540 parts, which leaves a shortage of

Delivery by: _____

Parts Delivery Table (May)

Issue date: April 22

	Delivery trips			Number of kanban	Difference from previous trip	Cases per day (1 case = 10 units)								Total part units for month of May
						1st	2nd	3rd		29th	30th	31st		
Part A	1	14	3	4	−1	8	8	0		8	8	8		1,718
Part B	1	14	3	3	0	6	5	0		5	5	4		1,020
Part C	1	10	2	3	−1	7	7	0		7	7	7		1,600
Part D	1	14	2	19	3	44	44	0		44	44	44		9,761
Part E	1	14	3	2	−1	5	5	0		5	5	5		1,141
Part F	1	10	2	1	0	1	0	0		1	0	0		94

Figure 7-4. Parts Delivery Table

sixty parts. To deliver these missing sixty parts, we could add an extra case to the daily delivery total, but that would mean a surplus of 160 parts. Instead, we should make up the shortage by assigning six eight-case days and by spreading those days out during the month as every third or fourth workday.

TOYOTA GROUP VAN

Toyota has made a number of developments in building an information system for communicating with suppliers.

Several years ago, Toyota established a value-added network (VAN) to provide an on-line link with major Toyota Group parts manufacturers such as Nippondenso, Toyoda Boshoku, and Toyoda Automatic Loom Works. More recently, Toyota established an on-line network with its major auto body contractors, which includes Toyota Auto Body, Kanto Auto Works, and Daihatsu Motor.

Companies that are linked to Toyota via these kinds of networks now receive parts delivery tables and exchange other data by computer communications instead of by hand delivery of documents or magnetic tape.

NETWORK WITH AUTO BODY
MANUFACTURERS (TNS-B)

There used to be situations in which a parts manufacturer would receive a parts delivery table from Toyota for a certain month's production much sooner than it received the parts delivery table for the same car from the Toyota-affiliated auto body manufacturer. Toyota's recently established TNS-B communication network has enabled the delivery of such tables and other information to be synchronized when desirable, as in this case. These kinds of data have been unified within the TNS-B network's central data base.

PARTS TRANSPORT METHOD

The kanban system has led to more frequent delivery trips for parts suppliers. In response to rising transport costs, parts suppliers have decided to form a cooperative load-sharing system. Under this system, delivery trucks shared by two or more parts suppliers stop at several factories on their way to Toyota's delivery dock. This way, each supplier still makes frequent deliveries while making fewer trips of its own.

However, it is not always possible to work out a schedule for load-sharing because of Toyota's strict delivery time schedule for various parts. Consequently, the parts suppliers have organized a warehouse-type distribution center near the Toyota assembly plant that they can all deliver their parts to. A third-party transport company is responsible for delivering parts from the distribution center to the Toyota warehouse on an hourly basis in accordance with instructions written on the kanban cards.

The transport company's distribution center/warehouse holds one or two days of inventory. The transport company also passes on kanban to the parts suppliers.

The total number of delivery routes that would be required for all parts suppliers to deliver their goods directly to the Toyota assembly plant would number in the hundreds and result in unacceptably high transportation costs. The use of an intermediary warehouse, where parts are delivered and sorted before delivery to their destination assembly plants, has reduced the number of delivery routes to about ten. This third-party warehouse and delivery operation provides the additional benefit to parts manufacturers of serving as a distribution center for deliveries to clients other than Toyota.

TOYOTA'S SIS DEVELOPMENTS

Toyota's Strategic Information System is the overall TNS, which as shown includes subsystems such as the TNS-D network linking Toyota with its dealers, the TNS-O network linking Toyota with its overseas assembly plants and representative offices, the TNS-S network linking Toyota with its suppliers, and the TNS-B network linking Toyota with its body manufacturers. These subsystems function beautifully. As of this writing, however, Toyota operates these subsystems independently and has yet to integrate them. Toyota manager Ei'ichi Sumibe remarked in 1990 that the TNS is not yet fully completed. They intend to establish mutual interconnections among subsystems, building an overall system that will enable product orders from sales outlets to be processed and sent directly to the relevant parts suppliers as parts orders.

Currently, system managers must take an active part in transferring information between TNS subsystems. To integrate all of the subsystems into a single Toyota Group TNS, Toyota must: (1) stay abreast of developments in Open System Interconnection (OSI) technology as a promising standard communications protocol, (2) unify and standardize the business protocol being used in the Toyota Group, and (3) devote further investment in TNS development as part of its mid- to long-term management strategy.

MULTILAYERED, DECENTRALIZED
FACTORY CONTROL SYSTEM

This section describes Toyota's version of computer-integrated manufacturing (CIM). At Toyota assembly plants, the system takes the form of a multilayered, decentralized factory control system. This long term simply means that each factory includes several autonomous subsystems that mutually adjust and control factory operations. The multilayered, decentralized factory control system also goes by the name compatible autonomous decentralized system.

Figure 7-5 illustrates the multilayered control system used by Toyota Group member Kanto Auto Works. The Kanto system was almost identical to the one used at Toyota assembly plants. Since then, however, a new system has been introduced at Toyota and will be described later.

1. The head office has a mainframe (host) computer for clerical data processing and each factory has a minicomputer connected to high-speed digital (optical fiber) communication channels.

2. At each factory, the minicomputers are linked via high-speed digital (optical fiber) communication channels to separate workstations for production control of various processes (such as the auto body processes, painting processes, and assembly processes).

3. The process-specific workstations are also called "line computers" since they are used to control the production lines. The line computers are connected as master computers to several smaller programmable controllers (PCs) that function as service units in performing tasks such as reading cards, printing out data, and controlling connected industrial robots and *andon* (alarm lamp) systems.

The functions of the line computers are described in more detail in Figure 7-6. (See Note 2 in the reference section.)

The minicomputer for each assembly plant is kept in an office called the assembly line control (ALC) room. Once a day, the host computer at the head office sends these ALC minicomputers feed-in sequence schedules and vehicle specifications files. The minicomputers then carry out daily distribution of files containing production schedule data to the process-specific line computers.

Once the process-specific line computers receive the production schedule data files, they control the processes

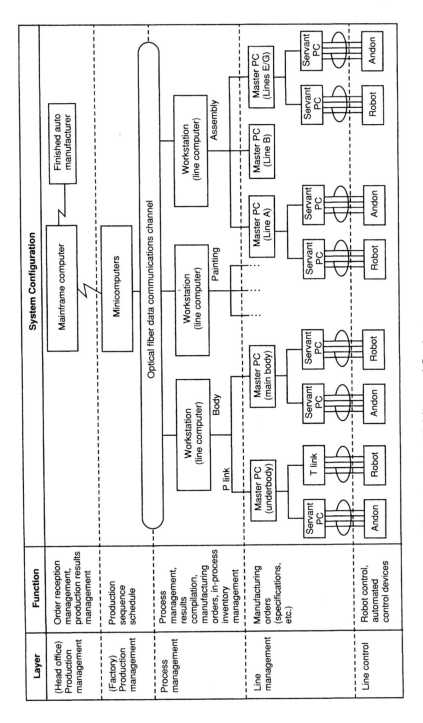

Figure 7-5. Computer Control Functions in a Multilayered System

independently and no longer rely upon the ALC room's minicomputer. Their only relationship with the minicomputer at this point is to send real-time progress report data to the ALC room.

Let us examine how process-specific control is carried out at the body assembly, painting, assembly, and inspection processes.

CONTROL SYSTEM FOR THE BODY ASSEMBLY PROCESS

The workstation (line computer) at the body assembly process issues body assembly work instructions for each vehicle in accordance with the feed-in sequence schedule. This workstation includes a printer that prints out cards to indicate the vehicle body identification (ID) numbers. Each card is attached to the vehicle body it identifies and is read by card-reader devices at various points during the body assembly process. The specifications for each vehicle body are obtained via a file search of the line computer's file. Then the specifications are output as work instructions that are sent to the factory center where conditions in the body assembly process are monitored.

A magnetic card printer at the start of the shell body line prints out magnetic ID cards for each vehicle on the line. (See the magnetic card example in Figure 7-7.) The magnetic card printer operates according to instructions sent from the ALC room. The vehicle ID card shows the car's model number and is attached to the car at the start of the shell body line. This magnetic card is *not* a kanban. It has a magnetic strip across the bottom, much like the magnetic commuter train tickets now used in some urban subway systems. As the vehicle makes it way down the car body line, its magnetic card is read at various stages by card-readers, which send the magnetic card's data to the ALC room to update the display monitoring each vehicle's progress on the line.

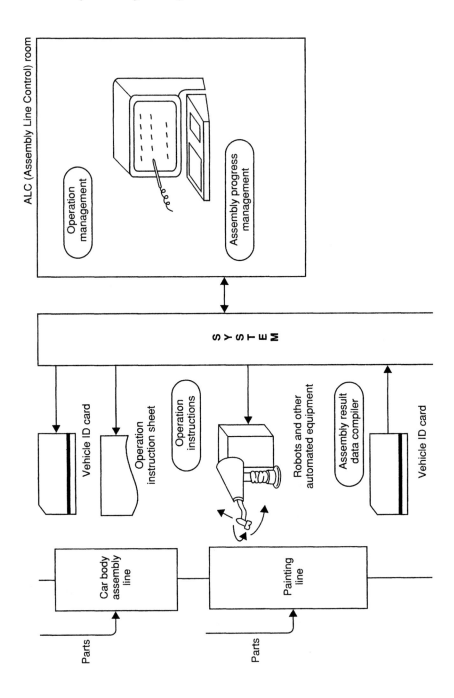

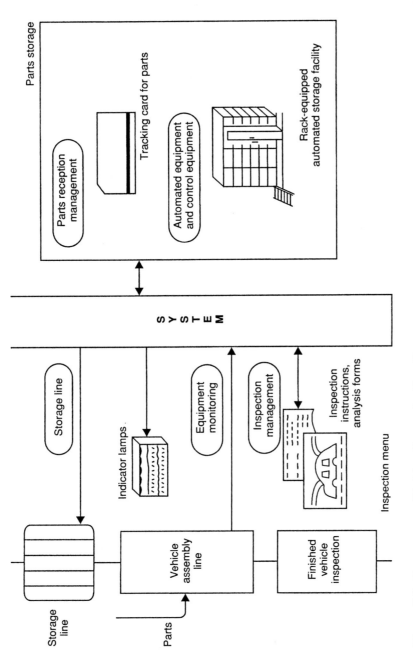

Figure 7-6. Process-specific Line Computer Functions

The line computer on the body line uses the factory line controller to issue vehicle ID cards and to control various equipment. For example, it selects the type of welding equipment needed according to the feed-in sequence and has that equipment brought to the side of the line in time to be used. It also manages the operation and changeover of automated body welding equipment that remains installed on the line.

CONTROL SYSTEM FOR THE PAINTING PROCESS

The painting process also utilizes card readers connected to the process-specific line computer, which prints out work instructions for the line workers based on the magnetic card data.

More recently, Toyota has introduced another type of card-shaped ID device that contains an integrated circuit (IC chip) and can transmit wireless signals. These cards are used to indicate the progress of vehicles passing through the painting process. The IC-based ID cards (also known as ID tags) have a much larger data memory capacity than magnetic cards have and are used in various assembly lines in addition to the painting line.

The industrial robots and other automated equipment on the line read their work instructions from each ID card's specification data.

Each vehicle's ID number corresponds to its body number. The ID card continuously transmits signals as it moves through the painting process and thereby indicates exactly how far the vehicle has come and when the painting process is finished. The ID card is highly resistant to heat and is not damaged when it gets painted along with its vehicle. After the painting process is finished, a worker shuts off the transmitter switch on the ID card.

The painting line operates under the following two types of sequence control:

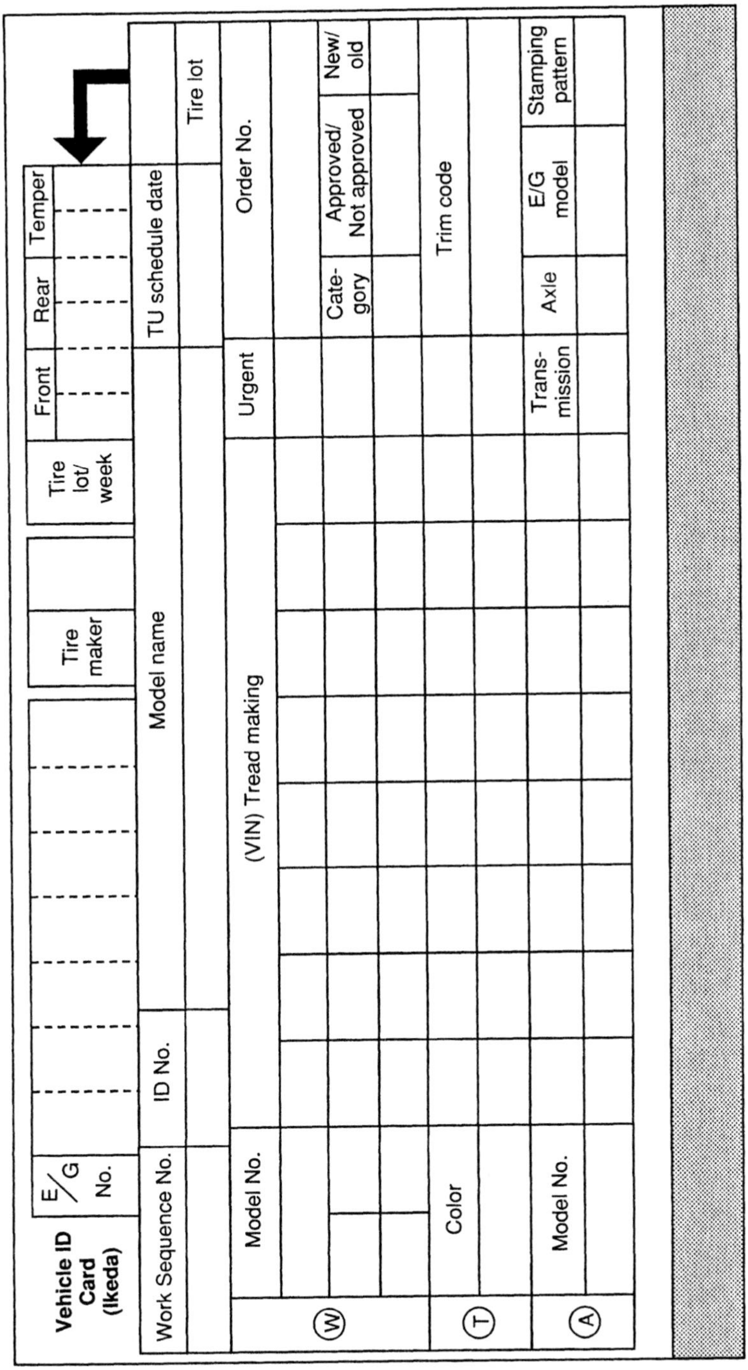

Vehicle ID Card (Ikeda)

E/G No.

Tire maker

Tire lot/week

Front | Rear | Temper

Work Sequence No.

ID No.

Model name

TU schedule date

Tire lot

Model No.

(VIN) Tread making

Urgent

Order No.

Category | Approved/Not approved | New/old

Trim code

W

Color

Transmission | Axle | E/G model | Stamping pattern

T

A

Model No.

Figure 7-7. Magnetic Card

The first type controls the feed-in and feed-out of car bodies to the storage line that is attached between the intermediate and final stages in the painting process. After the intermediate painting stage when the sequence of vehicles needs to be changed to obtain the maximum number of consecutive same-color car bodies in the final-stage painting booth, the sequence change is done in this storage line. This effectively cuts down on the number of paint color changeovers, which reduces both paint waste and changeover loss.

The second type of sequence control is feed-in and feed-out control of the painted-body storage line that follows the painting process. This storage line is used to change the order of vehicles before they enter the final assembly process. This is in response to real-time feed-in scheduling to obtain an optimum work-load balance on the final assembly line. Toyota employs an *expert system*, which is a computer system using artificial intelligence technology, to execute this sequential control.

The sequence in the painting line is susceptible to disruption due to the sorting out and repainting of car bodies that are found to have defective paint jobs. Repainting is always necessary for two-tone car bodies, and this makes sequential control quite complicated. When the car bodies exit the final stage in the painting process, freshly painted and suspended for drying, they must be put into the correct order for the final assembly line. The painted car bodies that enter the assembly process come from the painted-body storage line, where several painted car bodies are kept and their sequence rearranged.

Once the sequence of vehicles in the painted-body storage line has been worked out, the sequence information is input to the ALC room. The ALC room then sends the factory the corresponding sequence data for supplying engines and parts to the final assembly line.

Let us consider the Daihatsu assembly plant in Kyoto as an example. The Fuji Seat Company's factory is thirty minutes away from the assembly plant. Daihatsu's Shiga engine plant is an hour and a half away. However, after each vehicle enters the final assembly line, it takes two and a half hours to reach the engine installation stage. This allows enough time to order engine and seat supplies once the final assembly sequence has been determined.

CONTROL SYSTEM FOR THE FINAL ASSEMBLY LINE

As each vehicle is placed onto the final assembly line, a card reader reads its ID card and prints out a sticker with assembly work instructions.

The most recent type of work instructions used at Toyota and some other companies utilize symbols (such as pictures or single letters) instead of words to indicate the vehicle model and other assembly specifications. These symbols are stored as files in a data base. A different set of symbols is issued to each vehicle as it enters the assembly line. The use of such labels makes it easier for newer line workers to read and understand the work instructions quickly. Figure 7-8 illustrates some of the work instruction labels used at a Kubota tractor assembly plant.

The line workers at the start of the assembly line attach the label to the hood of the vehicle and the line workers downstream follow the label's instructions as they work.

The final assembly line includes nearly 100 stages and the variety of parts is mind-boggling — for example, there are thirty different types of speedometers. Since all of these options cannot be specified on a single label attached to the car's hood, additional labels are added downstream.

Working in parallel with this assembly line are various subassembly lines for engines, tires, seats, and other assembled parts. Work instructions for these subassembly lines are also read from the ID card and issued to their respective destinations.

In addition to the printing out of work instruction labels, a *multilayered electronic loop* operates a set of work instruction indicator lamps on the shelves where parts are stored. The electronic loop consists of a main workstation connected to several (from ten to 200) personal computers, all connected in a daisy-chain configuration via a twisted-pair cable. This loop operates sets of indicator lamps installed on parts storage shelves to show the line workers which parts to select. Sometimes, the loop is connected to devices that automatically select the indicated type and quantity of parts or materials and feed them to the assembly line. (See Figure 7-9.)

TOYOTA'S NEW ALC SYSTEM

Toyota first introduced its ALC system in 1966 and established a new ALC system in 1989 at its Tahara Plant. Since then it has introduced this new system to all of its other plants. (See Note 6 in the reference section.)

The design concepts behind this new ALC system naturally are based on the Toyota production system. They are intended to provide information on production needs on a just-in-time basis via a control system that is versatile and expandable.

These two systems — the ALC system and the Toyota production system — fit in with the multilayered, decentralized factory control system described earlier in this chapter. Toyota puts a strong emphasis on implementing the "pull system" approach to ensure a just-in-time flow of information.

Toyota uses an IBM mainframe as the head office's host computer. This mainframe is equipped with data-bank func-

Line	Serial No.	ID No.	Model Name	Model No.	Specs	Page Issue Date
003030	-3917	1070926	19202-00000 (110)	V1902	OEM 15 15- 47 47	0032 11 15
Engine slat			V1902B	63779		0001 / N CEA0403E 12 05

Cylinder head	Head gasket	Water temperature flag	Injection pump	Sym	Speed adjustment plate
Green	**G3**	V1902B	**Blue** (circled) / **Equipment**	Thickness = 2 / 0.45 = 2	15
Gear case	Stud for speed adjustment plate	Valve sheet	Water pump	Water flange	Steering / High idling
3	6 x 22 / 6 x 18	**Carrier**	**Carrier**	Installation — Short / Large / Existing	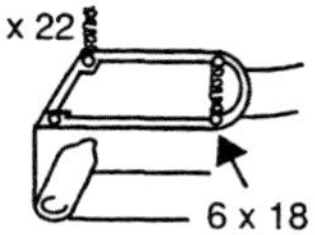   **Blue**
Fuel restrictions	Hour meter	Fuel pump	Engine hook	Jet cock	Inlet manifold / Glow plug
	Cover	**Cover** 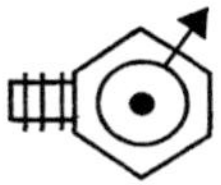 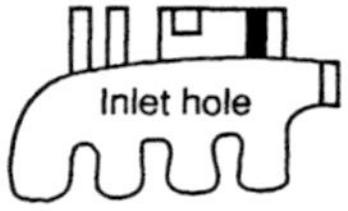		Long (exclusive)	Inlet hole 19202
Engine stop lever	Solenoid support	Fan-driven pulley	Oil gauge	Thermostat cover	Thermostat / Water drain

(Source: p. 37 of Takahashi, M. "Mixed Production of Truckter Factory," *Kojokanri*, Vol. 35. No. 1, Jan. 1989.)

Figure 7-8. Work Instruction Label

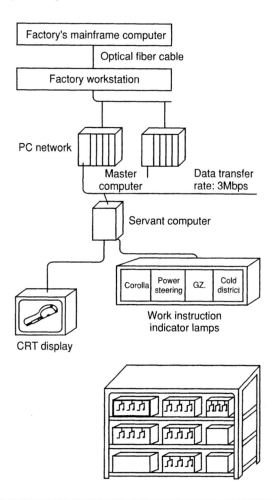

Figure 7-9. Work Instruction with Specification Indicator Lamps

	Work instruction indicator lamps	
	CRT display	Work instruction indicator lamps
Instructions	Screen display of color, shape, parts, etc.	Lamp display of model type, specifications, parts, symbols, etc.
	1 location	33 locations

tions for managing production information at all levels of the company.

Toyota establishes production sequence schedules that smooth out parts supply operations. All information regarding revisions and other changes to the schedule, as well as production results, are compiled and stored in the host computer's data banks. This system enables the head office to respond promptly to all information requests received from the company's factories and assembly plants.

The head office is also home to related information systems, such as for accounting (including cost calculation and budget management) and quality control. Toyota has made cross-referencing among these systems so easy that they are all virtually connected as one giant information system.

Please refer to Figure 7-10 as you read the following description of Toyota's new ALC system for issuing vehicle production work instructions.

The main computers at each Toyota plant are Fujitsu's FACOM-A-50 and FACOM-A-60. The FACOM-A-50 computer is connected via communication lines to the head office's IBM mainframe from which it receives data transmissions and performs communications protocol conversion. These functions make the FACOM-A-50 the plant's communications "gateway."

Data that have been converted by the gateway computer are input to the FACOM-A-60, which functions as a file server. Most of these data are parts of the production sequence schedule. The file server computer sends the head office mainframe requests for production information and manages the progress of vehicle production operations in its plant.

In Toyota's case, the process-specific line computers carry out various functions autonomously. Once a car body has received its ID tag, which is an ID unit that contains an IC card, the ID tag sends the file server a request for production

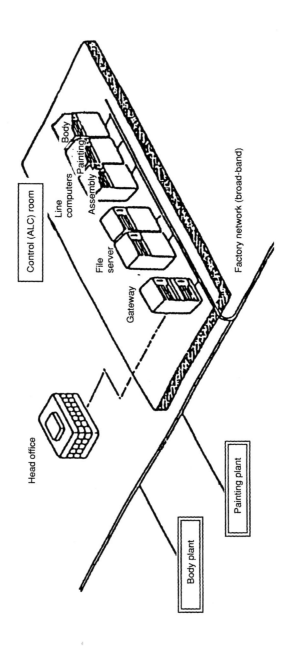

Control (ALC) room

Line
computers

Body

Painting

Assembly

File
server

Gateway

Factory network (broad-band)

Head office

Body plant

Painting plant

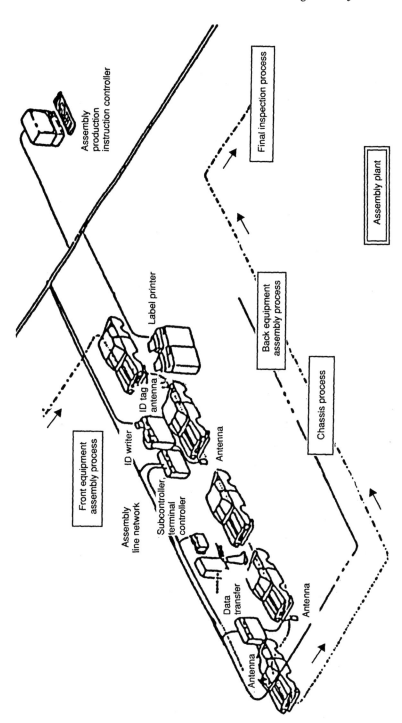

Figure 7-10. Overall View of the New ALC System

information. The file server sends the requested production information to the ID tag via the line's ID writer, which inputs the information into the ID tag. In this sense, the vehicle and the information are joined together in the line.

The most important characteristic of this new ALC system is that it works as a pull system in which each line and process in each plant requests, receives, and uses only the information it needs at the moment. As the vehicles make their way through the line, ID-tag antennas placed at strategic points on the line contact the ID tags and read information from them. This information is fed to the production work instruction controller, which controls the robots and other automated equipment on the line in accordance with the production work instructions.

JIT'S GOALS AND FRAMEWORK

The ultimate goal of the just-in-time production system is to make the entire company a profit-making operation. Therefore, JIT's basic objective is to reduce costs to aid profitability.

The goal of cost reduction and the goal of productivity improvement are largely the same thing. The key to achieving both goals is to thoroughly eliminate waste in all its forms, including excess inventory and excess labor.

We have been speaking of costs in very broad terms. In real terms, costs are the sum of past, present, and future cash outlays, all of which must be subtracted from total sales to determine whether or not a true profit has been achieved. These costs are referred to casually as the overall production cost, which properly includes not only the manufacturing costs but also sales expenses, general management expenses, capital costs, and other costs.

Many people think of JIT production as being mostly a matter of reducing inventory. Reducing inventory costs ties in directly with cutting capital costs, but these costs are classified as non-operating expenses and not as part of the manufacturing costs. However, reducing inventory helps expose hidden problems in the factory and solving these problems via small-group improvement activities can greatly reduce waste-related costs. Therefore, reducing inventory does tie in indirectly with cutting manufacturing costs.

Another indispensable part of cutting manufacturing costs is reducing manpower needs. Therefore, it is especially important that we understand the manpower reduction techniques used in the JIT production system. In fact, it is no exaggeration to say that reducing manpower costs is a more important part of JIT production than reducing inventory.

Within the framework of cost reduction, three subgoals must be achieved to make the main goal attainable:

1. *Volume management.* The scheduling of production output volume must be flexible on both monthly and daily bases in order to be responsive to market demand fluctuations.
2. *Quality management.* A system must be established that ensures that each process sends only nondefective goods to the next process.
3. *Respect the humanity of employees.* It is not possible to achieve the goal of higher productivity (nor that of lower costs) unless the company effectively develops the talents and skills of employees, instills enthusiasm in them, and respects their humanity.

How do these goals relate to the various levels of the JIT production system? Figure 7-11 outlines the overall framework of JIT production. This system contains an output (results) section that includes costs, quality, volume, and humanity and an input section that includes the company's constituent elements. Without getting into too much detail,

Figure 7-11 outlines the relationships among the various subsystems that make up the total system. We will discuss these subsystems one by one.

The first step is to eliminate inventory waste, manpower waste, and other waste in the factory to attain the goal of cost reduction. To do that, the management of production volume must be "flexibly responsive" to market demand fluctuations. This is a logical part of the JIT concept of making only the types and amounts of products that can be sold. When production line workers are also versatile enough in their skills to be able to switch from one line to the next as needed to meet fluctuating market demands, the result naturally will be a reduction in manpower-related waste.

JIT AND THE KANBAN SYSTEM

The goal of flexible production volume management can be reached if the concept of just-in-time production is well implemented. The JIT concept is summarized as producing *just what is needed, just in the amount needed, and just at the time it is needed.*

Toyota has developed and employed the kanban system as a system of daily production indicators and instructions that effectively implement the concept of just-in-time production. At Toyota, the monthly production schedule described earlier in the chapter plays a central role as a fairly accurate estimate of the next month's production requirements. As such, the monthly schedule for each production process is issued to all relevant processes and parts suppliers. The production schedule for the entire company is set with the help of a number-crunching computer, which in itself is admittedly a push production approach. However, the actual production instructions that come to each production process are issued by the final assembly line. They make their way upstream to

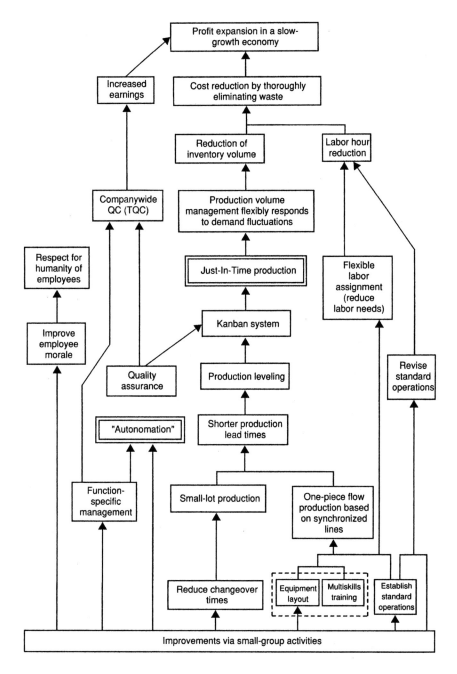

Figure 7-11. Outline of Toyota (JIT) Production System: How It Relates to Costs, Volume, Quality, and Humanity

earlier processes via kanban to ensure that only what is needed is sent downstream and only when it is needed. This is clearly a "pull production" approach.

Many people equate the Toyota production system with Toyota's famous *kanban* system. The two are not the same, however. The Toyota production system is group of practical methods for manufacturing products and the kanban system is a control method for ensuring just-in-time production. In other words, the kanban system is an information system that finely controls the volume and timing of production. Once all of the preconditions for the kanban system have been established (such as appropriate process design, standardized operations, and production leveling), some preliminary kanban are introduced to pave the way for full-fledged JIT production.

The Japanese word *kanban* means simply "signboard." This word was used for the system's kanban not because they are actual signboards but because they are indicators that, like signboards, require our attention.

Actually, kanban come in various shapes and sizes. Most are cards that slip into long plastic envelope-like holders. There are two main types of kanban: *withdrawal kanban* and *production kanban*. Withdrawal kanban indicate the amount of goods that the downstream process must withdraw from the previous (upstream) process. Production kanban indicate what kind of goods must be made at the previous process as well as their amounts. Kanban are cards that circulate within Toyota factories, between Toyota factories and their many parts suppliers, and also within the supplier factories. In this manner, kanban are the medium that carries information relating to the types and amounts of parts and products to be manufactured and supplied to achieve JIT production.

Let us imagine, for example, that an assembly line makes three product models A, B, and C. Parts a and b used to be manufactured on a machining line upstream as shown in Figure 7-12. Once machined, they are stored in an area behind the assembly line. Each lot of parts carries a production kanban from the assembly line.

A worker transports a set of withdrawal kanban from an assembly line geared up to assemble Model A to the machining line in order to withdraw the required number of part a's. At this point, the worker (1) exchanges the withdrawal kanban for boxes containing the exact number of part a's that the kanban indicate, (2) removes the production kanban attached to these boxes of parts, and (3) returns to the assembly line with this box of parts.

The production kanban that were removed are left at the kanban reception post at the parts store for the machining line. Because they represent a supply of parts that need to be resupplied, here they become production orders for the machining line. Remember — there is always one production kanban per box of parts.

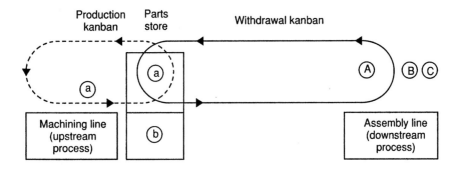

Figure 7-12. Flow of Two Types of Kanban

Actually, things are not quite this simple because the machining line in an actual factory constantly receive production-kanban resupply orders for both types of parts. However, this does not result in confusion. The machining line simply responds to the production kanban in the order they are received.

CONDITIONS FOR IMPLEMENTING
JIT PRODUCTION

To help the kanban system avoid sudden, impossible-to-meet demands for products from an upstream process or parts suppliers, factories must implement a technique called *production leveling* as a precondition for JIT production. In a nutshell, production leveling (or load smoothing) is the arrangement of mixed-flow production using several product models. This spreads out demand fluctuations among various types of parts, thereby dividing the impact of these fluctuations among several upstream sources. To implement this kind of mixed-flow production, a computer must be employed for the complicated task of figuring out the daily feed-in sequence for the final assembly line.

In turn, production leveling based on mixed-flow production can only work when there are short production lead times for all types of parts used in the products. (*Production lead time* is the time period between receiving a sales order for a product and shipping the finished product.)

The way to shorten production lead time is to produce all parts in small lots, if possible, using single-workpiece lots in a *one-piece flow production* and *one-piece conveyance* system. Although one-piece flow production is the ideal, it is more practical for some types of processes, such as press and forge processes, to handle small lots that do not exceed one day's output requirement for each part.

Small lot production rarely is achieved without reducing changeover times. Changeover operations are divided into (1) *external changeover*, or changeover that takes place while the process equipment is operating, and (2) *internal changeover*, or changeover that occurs while the process equipment is stopped. To shorten changeover time, we first turn as much internal changeover as possible into external changeover. We then find ways to shorten the times required for each type of changeover operations.

The key to achieving one-piece flow production lies in having production operations carried out by multiskilled workers who each handle a series of different processes, moving each workpiece through the series within a time period called the cycle time. Accordingly, we define *cycle time* as the amount of time needed to produce each product in order to meet the required daily output. To find the cycle time, we divide the operation time per day by the required daily output (the number of products needed per day). In JIT production, the required daily output is defined as the number of ordered products for that day. Consequently, cycle time is determined by the current market demands.

Another important precondition for one-piece flow production is what Toyota calls *standard operations*. At Toyota, standard operations includes the standardization of all operations that each of the line workers must perform in order to operate a series of processes within the cycle time. This combination of standardized worker operations is called *standard combinations*. Standard combinations make it possible to complete the manufacturing of each product within the cycle time.

METHODS FOR REDUCING LABOR-HOUR REQUIREMENTS

Next, the company must seek to cut costs by reducing labor-hour needs. The best way to do this is to establish flexible work assignments that enable the factory to add and subtract workers from lines in accordance with the demand fluctuations shown in the monthly production schedules. At Toyota, the concept of manpower reduction revolves around whether or not operators can be removed readily from lines that experience sudden demand drops.

One precondition for labor-hour reduction capability is reforming the equipment layout into *U-shaped cells*. It is especially beneficial to have a series of linked U-shaped cells so that reductions in demand can be accommodated more easily by reducing the number of U-shaped cell operators. Each U-shaped cell operator should be a multiskilled worker who is able to handle several different types of machines in accordance with the standard operation combination chart. In so doing, the operator should be able to operate all of the processes within his or her cell, making a full circle back to the first process within the cycle time.

QUALITY ASSURANCE METHODS

The kanban system is a key support for quality assurance. It clears away excess inventory and requires that the production line be stopped whenever defective goods appear one after another. In fact, the kanban system requires that only 100 percent defect-free goods be fed into and turned out of each stage of the production line.

One of Toyota's main quality control techniques is called *autonomation*, or "automation with a human touch." Autonomation is based on the development of mechanisms that can monitor production processes and detect abnormalities (defective goods or faulty production equipment). When these mechanisms detect an abnormality, they automatically stop the line and sound an alarm. Such devices help reduce manual labor and raise productivity.

After detecting an abnormality, the next step is to find and remove its root cause (usually, by making an improvement) so that the same abnormality does not recur. At Toyota, the improvements generally come from the company's suggestion system or from its small-group activities organization.

COMPANYWIDE IMPROVEMENT ACTIVITIES

The activities of QC circles and other small improvement groups include not only developing autonomation improvements but also improving changeover methods, standard operations, and other aspects of company operations. It is safe to say that small-group improvement activities comprise the most fundamental layer of support underlying the Toyota production system. The kanban system plays a large part in giving rise to the themes pursued by these improvement groups. It does so by eliminating inventory. Inventory tends to hide various types of problems — and less inventory means that more latent problems become apparent and demand solution by small-group improvement activities.

At the same time, the improvements made by these small groups motivate group members, who are ordinary factory workers. Improvement activities not only boost worker morale but also reiterate the company's respect for the humanity of workers as creative problem-solvers.

The Toyota production system also includes companywide quality control and cost control programs that encompass everything from product planning and design to production engineering (such as equipment capacity planning and production operations) and sales activities. After all, the overall goal of the production system is not so much quality control within the narrow confines of individual company departments as it is across-the-board improvement in corporate performance and profitability. To achieve this goal, the Toyota production system targets specific functions such as quality assurance and cost reduction and calls for regular function-specific conferences that cut across departmental boundaries with a view toward improving the overall company's performance of the function in question. Toyota calls this function-specific management.

CHAPTER 8

International Production Strategies
of Japanese Automakers

THE PAST DECADE has seen a conspicuous internationalization trend among Japan's automakers. The purpose of this chapter is to analyze the international production strategies taken thus far and to predict what course this internationalization trend is likely to take in the future.

First, let us clarify what we mean by internationalization. Some people think that merely exporting cars overseas is internationalization, while others draw the line at setting up sales companies and after-sales service centers overseas. One could even say that selling imported foreign cars is enough to make Japan's automotive industry "international." Here, however, our definition of internationalization is restricted to cases where Japanese automobile companies and automotive parts companies have set up production operations overseas, either to assemble and market finished automobiles or as suppliers of engines and other components to local automobile companies. In other words, we will focus on Japanese automotive companies that have shifted some of their production and parts procurement operations overseas as part of an international production and procurement strategy.

In the case of automakers, the costs and expertise required for overseas operations is enormous. The scope includes not only production operations *per se*, but also the construction of plants, the installation of equipment, the hiring of employees, and the development of supplier relationships. The various obstacles that lay in the path of setting up production overseas take a lot of time and effort to clear, and Japanese automakers cannot look upon overseas expansion of production as simply a matter of transplanting their domestic production systems overseas. Although they have built their success in Japan on home-grown practices such as the kanban system and affiliated supplier relationships, when moving such practices overseas these companies must be flexible and sensitive to the numerous issues related to international trade friction. Our discussion of international production strategy will also touch upon these trade issues.

The automotive industries in North America, Western Europe, and Japan are all mature industries that face a challenging future of limited growth amidst saturated domestic markets. Automakers in these countries must look to newer markets — such as in Eastern Europe and Asia — for growth potential. We will see how the international expansion strategies being employed by Japanese automakers in important markets such as North America, Korea, Taiwan, and other countries compare with the strategies of their U.S. and European competitors. We will study the goals that Japanese automobile companies have set for themselves in their overseas expansion of production and procurement. We will see what strategies they have adopted in pursuit of those goals and what their strategies are for the future. We will draw a relationship pattern describing the characteristics of various automakers in their international production and procurement strategies and study their direct production operations overseas.

OVERVIEW OF INTERNATIONAL PRODUCTION AND PROCUREMENT

There are advantages and disadvantages to each automaker's internationalization strategy and some of the problems encountered. Six categories will be examined:

1. the acquisition of overseas companies
2. the establishment of joint-venture companies overseas
3. contracted production
4. technology transfer
5. Original Equipment Manufacturer (OEM) production
6. independent expansion

These categories all involve situations in which Japanese automakers are setting up shop in countries that already have well-developed automotive industries — such as Western Europe, North America, and South Korea. Our first case study concerns a company that independently has built and operated its own overseas production facilities. The second describes a company that formed a joint venture with a local automaker to build new production facilities. The third looks at a company that bought out a local company and used its existing production facilities. The fourth looks at indirect overseas production expansion through contracted production at a local company's facilities. The fifth looks at technology transfer between a Japanese and a local company. Finally, the sixth case study looks at a Japanese automaker that accepts supplies of finished and semifinished products from a local automaker. We will begin with the cases that show the strongest connections between Japanese and local automakers. The final case study involves the expansion of a Japanese automaker into a developing country.

ACQUISITION

The acquisition strategy refers to a foreign automaker buying out a local automaker lock, stock, and barrel and then setting up production and procurement operations using that company's existing facilities.

Recent major examples of this strategy include the acquisition of the British automobile company Lotus by America's General Motors (1986), Italy's Maserati by America's Chrysler (1986), Spain's Seatto by Germany's Volkswagen (1986), Italy's Lamborghini by America's Chrysler (1987), and Britain's Jaguar by America's Ford (1989). There also have been acquisitions by same-country automakers, such as Alfa Romeo's acquisition by Fiat in Italy (1986) and American Motors by Chrysler in the United States (1987).

The buyers in these transactions have been America's "Big Three" (GM, Ford, and Chrysler) and some of Europe's biggest automobile companies (Volkswagen and Fiat). Note also that all of the acquired companies are small-scale manufacturers who boast a long tradition of excellent engineering in certain speciality fields, such as sports cars or four-wheel-drive vehicles. Recently, major automakers have been acquiring not only smaller automakers but also companies that specialize in various high-tech fields, such as computers or robotics.

With so many acquisitions occurring in recent years, we can assume that there must be some strong advantages in this strategy. Perhaps the greatest benefit is that acquisition is the fastest way to expand production to a new location. When one automaker buys out another, it acquires production facilities that have been operating for a long time, trained employees, production equipment, and a technological tradition that lives on in the engineering staff. These things are waiting and ready to go as soon as the acquisition deal is signed. In contrast to cases where one company uses another independent company's production facilities with little or no capital participation, a full-fledged acquisition enables the new owner to implement its own management strategy with complete freedom and maximum effectiveness.

Now, what is the downside? First, there is the question of financial risk. Needless to say, it takes a lot of money to buy out an automobile company, and the risk of not recovering the full investment rises dramatically if the buyer finds the actual benefits of the deal to be less than expected or has trouble implementing new management policies. In addition, even small automakers have considerable impact on local employment and local auto parts suppliers, and the local citizenry may be adverse to buy-outs. Generally, these factors alone have been enough to dissuade Japanese automakers from buying out overseas companies.

The following categories of overseas production strategies — namely, joint ventures, contracted production, original equipment manufacturer (OEM) production, and technology transfer — all involve some kind of tie-up with another automobile company. While tie-ups between automakers are nothing new, in recent years they have become increasingly subtle and complicated.

JOINT-VENTURE PRODUCTION

This category includes cases where a foreign automaker joins with either a local automaker or with another foreign automaker from the same country to establish a joint-venture plant.

Looking at the "Japanese partner" column in Table 8-1, we can see that in most cases, the Japanese partner is one of Japan's smaller automakers, such as Isuzu, Subaru, Suzuki, and Mitsubishi. This makes sense in light of the fact that the chief advantage of joint-venture expansion is that its investment cost burden is roughly half that of direct expansion of production. In addition, the two partners share the investment risk. Another advantage is that the two partners get to share each other's production management skills and expertise. Looking at the joint-venture company, NUMMI, established by Toyota and General Motors, Toyota's strategy was to share the investment risk while testing the waters for possible further expansion of production in North America on its own in the future. NUMMI also provides Toyota with an invaluable opportunity to study firsthand how American automobile plants are managed and how labor-management relations are handled.

Table 8-1. Major Joint-venture Production Between Japanese and Western Automakers

Japanese Partner(s)	Western Partner	Target Country	Production Start	Production Capacity	
Toyota	GM	U.S.A.	1985	250,000 vehicles per year	Provides finished cars to both partners
Mitsubishi	Chrysler	U.S.A.	1988	240,000 vehicles per year	Provides finished cars to both partners, scheduled to switch over to Chrysler engine production in the future
Suzuki Motors	GM	Canada	1989	200,000 vehicles per year	About 80% of output goes to GM
Isuzu and Subaru		U.S.A.	1990	240,000 vehicles per year	Provides finished cars to both partners
Isuzu	GM	Britain	1990	40,000 vehicles per year	Produces commercial vehicles only
Honda	British Rover	Britain	1991	100,000 vehicles per year	Provides finished cars to both partners

On the other hand, there are disadvantages in joint-venture production. First, there is the fact that the smaller the investment risk is, the smaller the potential for profit. Joint ownership also makes the prompt expansion of production output of popular automobile models more difficult. Also, even though investment costs are only about half of what they would be if the foreign company set up shop on its own, these costs are still much higher than for contracted production or other alternatives. Moreover, it takes longer to move from the planning stage to full-fledged production when there are two companies involved. This longer lead time boosts investment costs. Both companies must take the necessary time and effort to work together as partners. This is not only during the planning and construction phases, but also when dealing with the inevitable problems that arise during regular production operations — such as labor relations and local procurement policies.

CONTRACTED PRODUCTION

Contracted production usually take the form of a foreign automaker providing capital and/or technology or joint research & development to a local automaker in exchange for producing cars to be sold under the foreign automaker's brand. This differs from OEM production in which one company's finished automobiles or components (such as engines) are used to fill a gap in another company's product line-up. The client company has no real input into the planning and production of those vehicles or components. By contrast, in contracted production, the client is always involved to some extent in developing the products it receives from the contracted company.

Let us look at some recent examples of contracted production. Our first example is a tie-up between Honda and Britain's Rover Group. In this case, Rover was contracted to produce 4,000 Honda Ballade models per year beginning in 1986. The next step concerned other models, such as the Honda Legend, which were jointly developed by Honda and Rover. The agreement was that Rover would produce all of these models destined for the European market at its own plants.

Another joint venture was made between Toyota and Volkswagen. Volkswagen was contracted to produce Toyota-brand small pickup trucks in then-West Germany for the European market. Meanwhile, in the United States, Nissan and Ford joined hands to develop several car models under both companies' brands to be produced at Ford plants for the U.S. market. Mazda also concluded a contract production deal with Ford to produce all of the Mazda-brand mini-pick-up models that previously had been exported from Japan to North America.

A common thread in all of these cases is that the Japanese partner provided technology and participated in joint product development that was restricted to certain specialized vehicle models and in relatively small volumes, with all vehicles to be marketed via the Japanese partner's sales channels. The advantages in this kind of contracted production deal are, first, that it eliminates the heavy cost and labor burden of building new production plants. Further, the small-scale production volume reduces the investment risks. Secondly, there is no need to enter sticky labor relations. The contracted automaker benefits from a boost in production and the introduction of new technology. In addition, these instances of contracted production help reduce trade friction.

The primary drawback is that these examples offer little potential for profit. However, when this disadvantage is weighed against such important considerations as the need to reduce trade friction and to cultivate better relations with overseas automakers, we can understand why Japanese automakers have made so many contracted production deals in a wide variety of specialized fields.

TECHNOLOGY TRANSFER

Many technology transfer arrangements have been made between Japanese automakers and (1) those in developing or newly developed countries such as South Korea and Taiwan or (2) small-scale automakers in Europe and North America. In every case, the automaker who receives Japanese automotive technology or investment capital already has established a solid manufacturing base that possesses a certain level of technical sophistication and production capacity.

Such technology and/or capital is intended to help the recipient company expand production capacity and boost productivity and product quality. This kind of arrangement is currently the only one politically feasible in countries (such as South Korea and Taiwan) that are not receptive to the idea of direct production expansion by Japanese automakers. The Japanese regard technology transfer as a way to get their feet in the door for possible contracted production or other tie-ups in the future.

One way in which technology transfer differs from contracted production is that the vehicles produced as a result of a technology transfer agreement are sold by the local company under its own brand, and all sales revenue belongs to the local company. The only revenue the Japanese company who provided the technology receives is indirect revenue, such as technology licensing fees and profits from sales of exported parts. The main point of technology transfers is to help recipient companies raise their productivity, hold down costs, and improve quality to a level on par with that of Japanese, European, and U.S. automakers.

Even before receiving Japanese technology transfers, some companies in South Korea and Taiwan had developed their technology to a level where they established a niche for themselves in the subcompact sector of the North American automobile market. As they benefit from ongoing technology transfers from Japan, these companies can look forward to becoming better established as full-fledged manufacturers in their own market niches.

OEM PRODUCTION

Original Equipment Manufacturer (OEM) production is defined as the production and delivery of entire finished vehicles or major components such as engines to another automaker that has not participated in the product's development or parts supply. The products are made completely by the supplier but are sold by the recipient under the latter's brand name. Usually, OEM production occurs when an automaker wants to market a type of vehicle that it is unable or unprepared to produce on its own. Recently, the most noteworthy examples of this have been cases in which one of America's Big Three automakers makes a deal with a Japanese, South Korean, or Taiwanese automaker to provide mass-market and subcompact models under an OEM arrangement. For instance, in the field of subcompact cars, GM has OEM deals with Japan's Isuzu and Suzuki and South Korea's Daewoo, Ford receives OEM cars from Japan's Mazda, South Korea's Kia, and Taiwan's Ford Ryuhua, and Chrysler has an OEM deal with Japan's Mitsubishi.

During the 1970s and 1980s, the Big Three responded to the fast-growing fuel-efficient subcompact and compact sectors of the U.S. market by launching programs to develop these types of cars. However, their lack of experience in these sectors, combined with high labor costs, has made success difficult. This prompted them to turn to a strategy of OEM production using Asia's low-cost subcompact automakers. In the 1980s, GM launched its Saturn project aimed at developing a new generation of compact car. By the time the first Saturn cars hit the market, however, GM had downscaled the project from half a million to 200,000 units and upgraded the Saturn's class ranking to the 2,000-cc level. (This is on par with the higher-ranked compact car class in Japan.)

In Japan, OEM production deals are not uncommon among domestic automakers. However, it is rare that an overseas automaker supplies OEM cars to a Japanese company. It is true that several Japanese car companies have purchased foreign-brand cars for sale in Japan, but these are not OEM deals — the Japanese merely are acting as import and marketing agents for the foreign-brand cars. Examples of this include the importation and sales of Germany's Opel cars by Isuzu, France's Peugeot cars by Suzuki, Sweden's Volvo cars by Subaru, and France's Citroen cars by Mazda. Nevertheless, it is possible that such arrangements may develop into OEM deals at some point in the future.

An advantage of OEM production is that the recipient company risks no investment in the production of the OEM cars and can remain flexible in renewing or canceling its OEM deals from year to year. OEM production also enables a car company to quickly introduce specialty models that it is not equipped to develop and produce on its own.

One drawback of OEM production is that OEM cars rarely fit in with the recipient company's overall design image.

Figure 8-1 illustrates the differences among the three strategies of contracted production, technology transfer, and OEM production.

DIRECT PRODUCTION EXPANSION

Direct production expansion occurs when a company acts on its own to set up production facilities in a new location, in

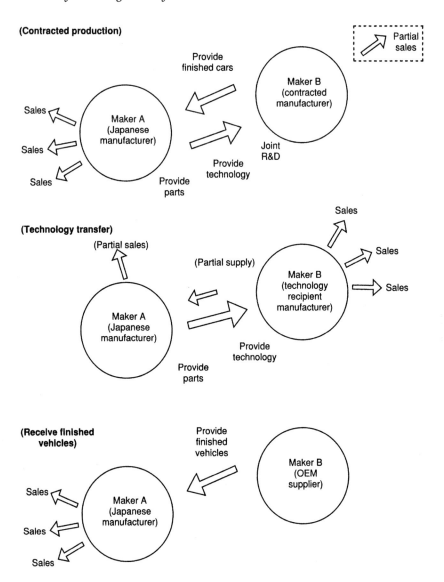

Figure 8-1. Differences Between Contracted Production, Technology Transfer, and OEM Production

this case overseas. Table 8-2 lists several cases in which Japanese automakers have directly expanded their production operations to North America and Europe during the 1980s to (1) reduce trade friction and (2) avoid higher domestic production costs resulting from a steep rise in the value of the yen.

The list of Japanese automakers that have directly expanded their production operations overseas is dominated by the bigger, more financially powerful companies — Toyota, Nissan, and Honda. The target countries, the United

Table 8-2. Major Examples of Direct Production Expansion by Japanese Automakers in Europe and North America

Company	Target country	Factory site	Production start	Annual production capacity	
Toyota	U.S.A.	Kentucky	1988	200,000 vehicles	Full-fledged production of engines slated for 1991.
Nissan	U.S.A.	Tennessee	1983	260,000 vehicles	In 1992, capacity will be raised to 400,000 vehicles and will start engine production.
Honda	U.S.A.	Ohio	1982	360,000 vehicles	Soon will have second plant, raising capacity to 510,000 vehicles. Already has begun engine production.
Mazda	U.S.A.	Michigan	1987	300,000 vehicles	Plans to produce engines also.
Toyota	Canada	Ontario	1988	50,000 vehicles	
Honda	Canada	Ontario	1986	80,000 vehicles	
Toyota	Britain		1992	200,000 vehicles	Plans to produce engines also.
Nissan	Britain	Tyne-and-Ware	1986	100,000 vehicles	Already has begun engine production.

States, Canada, and Britain, are major automobile markets that are most likely to support the large-scale local production of Japanese cars.

The advantages of this strategy are centered on the greater potential for profit that comes with such large-scale production and capital investment. The fact that these companies are going it alone in their expansion projects gives them the freedom to make rapid changes in production scale and planned vehicle models in response to changing conditions. Having local production facilities also has spin-off benefits such as improving the company's image in the local market.

As for the disadvantages, the huge investment required for large-scale direct overseas production creates a major financial risk for the company, which has a big impact on the company's management. The company must be prepared to spend many years in detailed planning and preparations before beginning production overseas. In addition, establishing large-scale production that does not include tie-ups with local automakers introduces a new major competitor on the local market, and this can create a new kind of trade friction.

EXPANSION TO DEVELOPING COUNTRIES

Let us now consider cases in which automakers from major industrialized countries expand production to developing countries. When looking into this strategy, companies must consider the need to transfer manufacturing technology, some elements of the industrial infrastructure that may be missing in the target country, as well as the legal restrictions imposed by the target country on imported automotive products and direct investment. These factors, plus the fact that the typical developing country cannot offer a major market for automobiles, make it difficult for automakers to see any overall merit in this strategy.

Therefore, investing in developing countries, both large and small, has not been direct and independent. Instead it occurs within the framework of a consortium of companies, consisting perhaps of an automaker, a machinery manufacturer, and a financial institution, who together help build factories and provide financial assistance, install modern production equipment, and/or extend technical aid to a local automobile company. In any case, the amount of investment and scale of expansion are generally small, the project being shaped more by industrial and economic conditions in the target country than by the needs of the investors. There is no point in discussing the problems posed by different project formats.

Problems often encountered when attempting to operate these types of factories include inefficient production and low profitability due to the factories' small scale, unforeseen problems in parts procurement due to the underdeveloped state of local parts suppliers, a low level of education and skills among local workers, and restrictions imposed by the target country's government. Some countries also pose a large investment risk due to their political instability.

On the other hand, many developing countries receive preferential treatment in trade relations and other industry-boosting assistance. Any foreign automaker that helps such countries develop a stable, high-quality automotive industry can look forward eventually to enjoying a relatively low-cost production and procurement environment with potential for long-term growth.

FUTURE DIRECTION OF INTERNATIONAL PRODUCTION AND PROCUREMENT STRATEGIES

Having examined several major examples of international production and procurement strategies undertaken by

Japanese automakers, let us look at which direction these strategies are likely to take for the future.

THE OUTLOOK FOR INTERNATIONAL TIE-UPS BETWEEN AUTOMAKERS

We have already considered examples of Japanese automobile companies working with automobile companies in North America, Europe, South Korea, and Taiwan in three kinds of tie-ups: joint-venture production, contracted production, and OEM production. What directions might these strategies take in the future?

DIRECTION 1 One direction is to make further progress in the international division of industry among companies. This means that manufacturers in various countries assume a greater share of operations for products or production processes in which they are especially competitive, such as in terms of their technological level in production, R&D, or their labor-cost advantage. The result is a global division of industry whose products are shipped to every market.

An example of the process-specific division of industry is when one country's automaker produces engines and other major components for various car models while a company in another country assembles the components into finished cars. An example of product-specific division of industry is when an automaker in one country sticks to its specialty of mass-market economy cars while one in another country turns out only luxury cars. This international division of industry has been pursued to some extent by Ford, General Motors, and Chrysler in the United States. It is a direction that involves some degree of capital participation among the member companies, and it is possible that the global auto industry will shift more in this direction as a way to ensure its survival amidst an increasingly competitive business environment.

The two categories of process-specific and product-specific division of industry are mixed in the current international industrial division as illustrated in Figure 8-2. The product-specific category can be seen in the case of subcompact cars being supplied to GM by Isuzu and Suzuki and to Chrysler by Mitsubishi. In this case, Japan is the country that currently shows the highest degree of competitiveness in the design, development, and manufacture of small economy cars. As for the process-specific category, this can be seen in the case of automotive components for certain car models in North America being supplied by South Korean manufacturers who have received technical guidance from their U.S. clients.

As a worldwide international division of industry is created, this trend may continue not only with regard to subcompact cars and other economy cars but also in the field of luxury cars. We have already seen cases of luxury cars being made for other companies, such as in Ford's luxury-car export sales in Japan via Mazda, Opel's via Isuzu, and GM's via Suzuki. If profitable, these arrangements may develop into OEM deals in the future.

As automobile companies in South Korea and Taiwan continue to receive technology transfers, contracts for supply of parts and small cars suddenly may shift from Japan to these countries to take advantage of lower production costs. This shift already has begun at the most internationally diversified group centered on the Ford Group, as Mazda already imports and sells (in Japan) Ford cars manufactured in Taiwan. Meanwhile, South Korean automaker Hyundai is working hard to raise its technology level and already supplies parts to Mitsubishi.

DIRECTION 2 Another strategic direction is the increasingly cut-and-dried, unsentimental nature of tie-ups among automakers. Automotive groups no longer stay so much

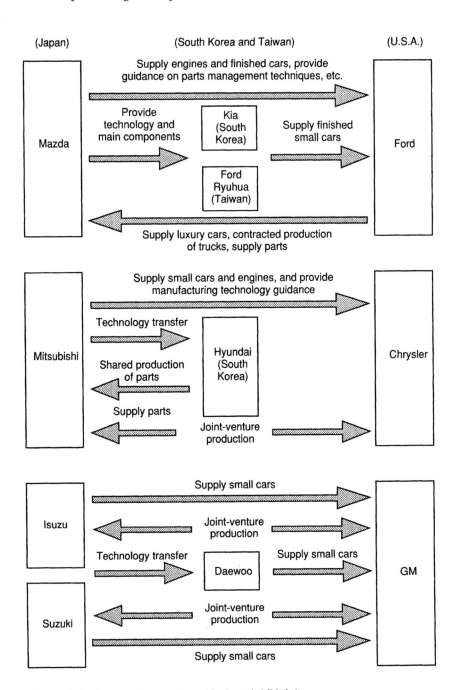

Figure 8-2. Current International Industrial Division

within the framework of their traditional supplier networks. Nowadays, they simply look for the best deal — even if it means joining forces with a domestic or overseas competitor.

It used to be that going outside the traditional supplier network was something only Western automakers would consider — Japanese companies remained firmly bound to their affiliated supplier system. However, Toyota was the first to break with tradition by entering into joint-venture production with GM in the United States. As the world's first and second largest automakers, they were the ultimate rivals in the automotive industry. But as explained earlier, Toyota recognized the joint-venture project as an opportunity to gain experience in U.S.-based production that could prove invaluable later on if Toyota decided to build production facilities on its own there.

GM also jumped at the opportunity to boost its small-car production while studying firsthand the legendary Toyota production system, noted for its excellence in production control, parts management, and quality control. In addition to its ties with Toyota, the GM Group has also made parts-supply arrangements with Nissan as well as commercial-vehicle production ties with Nissan via South Korea's Daewoo.

Consider also the case of Germany's Volkswagen, which has a tie-up with Toyota for commercial-vehicle production in Germany and with Toyota's main rival Nissan with regard to passenger cars. Such is the rational and completely unsentimental nature of today's global automotive industry. There are more examples: Nissan has an agreement with Ford concerning U.S.-based production of multipurpose vehicles while Ford continues to have a strong and wide-ranging relationship with Mazda in the areas of subcompact and mass-market economy cars.

Perhaps the most surprising break from the strongly group-oriented corporate tradition in Japan came when the small-scale automakers Isuzu and Subaru announced they were going to set up joint production facilities in the United States. After all, Isuzu already had been associated with the GM Group and Subaru with the Nissan Group. This did not prevent these two small companies from joining forces to improve their opportunities in the high-risk, mammoth-investment project of setting up a production plant in the United States. As one last example, we should note that broad-ranging tie-ups have been established in Australia between Toyota and GM and between Nissan and Ford.

As we can see, automakers in various countries have decided to transcend several boundaries, including corporate groupings and national borders, in a rational pursuit of tie-up arrangements that will help relieve trade friction and enable each company to concentrate on its strengths and compensate for its weaknesses in the global automotive market. We can expect similar tie-ups, based on certain car models, parts, or regional markets, to be even more common in the future.

OUTLOOK FOR OVERSEAS PRODUCTION FACILITIES

In examining the role of the independent or joint-venture establishment of overseas production facilities in the international production and procurement strategies of Japanese automakers, we will focus on the size and strategic importance of overseas production facilities in Europe and North America.

THE FIRST TREND

First, we can expect to see an increasing use of overseas plants to produce cars exported to a third country. For example, Japanese auto plants in Britain have been built to turn out cars not only for the British market but also for the European Community.

By contrast, Japanese auto plants in the United States and Canada have been intended to supply only the U.S. and

Canadian markets. A U.S.-Canadian automobile trade agreement has established standards for duty-free exportation and importation of automotive parts between the two countries. This bilateral agreement already has allowed a limited range of finished car import/export, a range that is expected to broaden in the future. However, considering that the Canadian market is dwarfed by the size of the U.S. market and has no automobile companies of its own, and in view of the two nations' geographical and cultural similarities, it is possible to treat the U.S. and Canadian automotive markets as one market. Although the Japanese auto plants in the U.S. and Canada began by serving only the U.S./Canadian market, some cars produced at these plants are now exported to third countries and it is likely that more will be exported to Europe or elsewhere in the future.

One case in point is NUMMI, the Toyota-GM joint venture in California that has begun exporting Corollas to Taiwan. The NUMMI Corollas exported to Taiwan are, in terms of technology and model class, ranked one step below the Corona models that are manufactured in Taiwan by Kouzei under a technology transfer agreement with Toyota. Another instance is Honda America, which now exports some of its Accord models to South Korea. In addition, Chrysler and Mitsubishi plan to export sports cars made at their American joint-venture plant to Europe. One factor that lies behind all of these third-country export strategies is the array of restrictions that various countries have placed on Japanese automotive imports in the wake of mounting trade friction. Japanese companies have used, and will continue to use, the pattern of third-country exports from U.S.-based production plants as one way to work within these restrictions. They still face various trade pressures, however, such as the call for a higher ratio of locally procured parts.

A SECOND TREND

Other growing trends in overseas production include the "reverse import" phenomenon in which finished or semifinished vehicles are produced at Japanese auto plants overseas and then exported to Japan, while engine or other major component production is divided among two or more overseas plants. This strategy enjoys the double advantage of helping to alleviate trade friction while enabling more flexible responses to currency exchange fluctuations.

The first case of Japanese reverse imports came in 1987 when Honda began importing Accords from its Ohio plant. Mitsubishi followed suit in February 1990 when it began importing sports cars from the Chrysler/Mitsubishi joint-venture plant in the United States. The engines and some other major components in these cars were supplied previously from Japan. By the time the reverse imports began, however, the joint-venture plant had begun receiving the engines and components from other overseas plants. Also by 1987, the Nissan plant in Smyrna, Tennessee, had begun receiving engines from Nissan's plant in Mexico. This strategy helped ease trade tensions while avoiding the effects of the high yen and taking advantage of the two plants' relative proximity. More recently, the Japanese government began considering the idea of making it obligatory for Japanese automakers to establish overseas production to meet a minimum level defined as a percentage of their export volume.

As this trend continues, we will begin to see individual companies carry out their own international division of industry. It is even possible that Japanese automobile companies may assign all production for certain car models to overseas plants, from which they will be imported in reverse to Japan. Something approximating this has already occurred in the case of the sports cars that Mitsubishi imports to Japan from the Chrysler/Mitsubishi plant. Mitsubishi has never produced these cars in Japan. In addition, Mazda already has made plans to have certain sports car models produced only in America and to supply the Japanese market by reverse imports. Nissan is working out an international division of labor among its plants in Japan, the United States, and Britain for certain car models. Figure 8-3 compares the previous pattern of manufacturing and exporting with the pattern that is taking shape today.

A THIRD TREND

A third trend worth noting is the shift toward greater independence for overseas plants. There has been a slow but steady transfer of authority from automobile company head offices in Japan to their overseas companies. This shift concerns not only decision-making authority but also the ratio of local managers to Japanese managers and the percentage of profits channeled back into the local company. Decision-making authority is being increased for overseas company managers in the area of production management as well as in other areas, such as management at subsidiaries and dealerships, marketing, and even research and development. We can expect such local independence to become even more prominent in the future.

As an example, in 1989 Toyota established its U.S. head office and transferred all of its equity in U.S.-based Toyota subsidiaries to that head office. It also gave its U.S. company the authority to manage and operate local Toyota factories, to plan marketing and sales strategies with local dealerships, and to coordinate and act as a liaison between Toyota-affiliated companies in the United States and Toyota in Japan.

Honda, the first Japanese automaker to establish production facilities in North America, has since created an independent

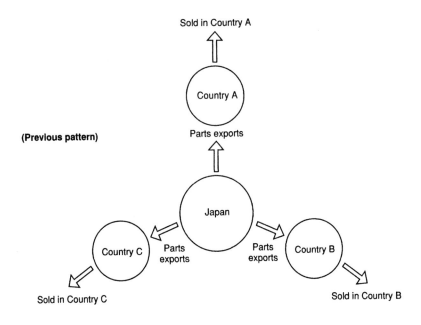

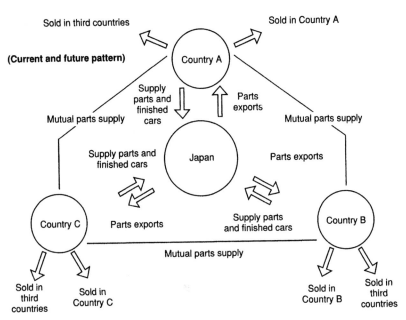

Figure 8-3. Development of Manufacturing and Exporting Trends

company, Honda North America, for both U.S. and Canadian markets. This company is now recognized widely both in Japan and North America as an independent local company. It has demonstrated this independence by moving on its own to build a second assembly plant. The Accords that are reverse-imported to Japan are advertised proudly as "Made in U.S.A." Honda North America makes every effort to demonstrate its success to North Americans as a successful local company. In this regard, Honda has moved beyond the strategy of an international division of labor to emphasize a strategy of making its overseas companies so strongly independent that they begin to compete with Honda in Japan.

Realizing that local developers are in closer touch with the preferences of local consumers, Japanese companies have begun to set up product development departments in their overseas companies. These overseas development departments are linked via a communications network with their counterparts in Japan to create a more efficient product development system.

PROBLEMS AND ISSUES CONCERNING OVERSEAS PRODUCTION

This section looks at various problems and issues that have arisen as Japanese automakers carry out the overseas expansion strategies described in the previous section, including independent expansion and joint-venture expansion. We will focus mainly on examples of overseas expansion in the United States. The two issues that have been most critical in determining the success or failure of overseas production facilities are local content ratio (the percentage of parts procured from local companies) and labor relations. Other less critical issues include methods for training workers, social relations within the local community, and local perceptions regarding the Japanese staff. After describing these issues, we will see how Toyota has worked to solve them.

PROBLEMS AND ISSUES CONCERNING
THE ESTABLISHMENT OF
OVERSEAS PRODUCTION FACILITIES

Local content is a pressing issue for Japanese companies that independently have set up production facilities overseas. Since beginning production operations, these companies have tried to raise the local content ratio in several ways. The growth in local production of Japanese cars and continued growth in imports have both contributed to the growing share Japanese-brand cars enjoy in the U.S. market. This share expansion has resulted in stronger demands for increasing the local content ratio.

In addition, a strong adverse reaction has been witnessed regarding the increasing numbers of Toyota and Nissan cars reaching European markets from production facilities in Britain. Toyota and Nissan face stiff opposition to this strategy of expanding their EC market shares via production bases in EC-member Britain, especially from France and other protectionist-prone European nations. The latter are seeking to impose a requirement that all cars must have a local content ratio of at least 80 percent to be recognized as EC-produced cars.

There are three ways to achieve such a high local content ratio. One way is to have the EC-based factories (in Britain, in this instance) get 70 or 80 percent of the parts from either in-house production or local suppliers. However, since most local suppliers have neither the technology nor the right equipment to provide major components such as engines and transmissions, the Japanese companies would have to manufacture these components in-house. However, in-house production would require huge investments of capital, and there probably would not be enough demand to make such investment profitable.

A second way is to buy parts from local manufacturers. After deciding that this would be the most effective approach since it would also help alleviate trade friction, Japanese companies began pursuing this policy. However, in so doing, they found that local parts manufacturers either were unable to meet their quality and delivery requirements or were unable to provide the needed parts. These problems, plus logistical and geographical ones, posed a major obstacle to recreating a Japanese-style production system that is based on the existence of top-quality parts suppliers. Rather than forcing the Japanese production system down the suppliers' throats, Japanese companies introduced technical guidance programs and recognized the need for flexibility in response to local conditions.

A third way to raise the local content ratio is to buy parts from Japanese suppliers who have also set up shop overseas. Recognizing the demand for their higher-quality and more technologically advanced auto parts, growing numbers of Japanese suppliers have set up overseas factories near their traditional clients. Naturally, a large influx of Japanese suppliers would not be welcomed by the local suppliers. To avert this kind of trade friction, many Japanese suppliers are establishing joint-venture factories with local companies.

In labor relations, there are big differences between Japanese and European/North American cultures with regard to racial identity, social customs, and attitudes toward work. These differences make it difficult to take a Japanese-style production system premised upon multiskilled workers, QC circle activities, and standard operations and apply it elsewhere. Japanese automakers setting up production facilities in the

West must work first to gain understanding from local managers and workers regarding the company's management
methods and its Japanese-style production system and labor
relations policies. In the United States in particular, the major
stumbling block for Japanese companies in their labor relations has been reaching an understanding with the automotive
industry's giant labor union — the United Auto Workers
(UAW). Japanese managers realized that it was essential to
reach an agreement with the UAW regarding Japanese-style
labor relations.

Another important issue is personnel training. Efficient
production operations depend upon a personnel training program that teaches local employees the multiple skills needed
for their new jobs. Other important issues include the need
for the company to contribute to the local community and to
establish good social relations with people in the community.
This ties in with another need, which is to establish good
employer/employee relations with local workers, and to
obtain their trust and encourage their loyalty and enthusiasm
for the company. These human factors contribute much to the
quality of products and to the efficiency of plant operations. It
is important for overseas enterprises to approach these social
and human factors carefully.

HOW TOYOTA SET UP SHOP OVERSEAS

Let us examine how Toyota dealt with the kinds of
issues just described when it established production facilities overseas.

First, how did Toyota establish its local parts supply network? Toyota had set a local content target of 60 percent
when it started its new plant in Kentucky. One of the many
reasons why Toyota chose Kentucky as the site for its plant
was because it was close to Detroit, America's automotive

capital. It was within sufficiently close range of not only the traditional Detroit parts manufacturers but also the manufacturers who were already supplying parts to other Japanese-run factories in the area. As part of its effort to use as many local parts suppliers as possible, Toyota contacted about 1,200 auto parts companies before opening its factory, selected sixty companies that appeared to have the needed levels of technology and product quality, and then began organizing its local parts procurement system.

In an attempt to recreate the kind of parts production and delivery system it has in Japan, Toyota sent engineers to help parts suppliers gear up for Toyota's needs such as developing new parts to meet Toyota's specifications. Toyota also planned meetings every six months, bringing representatives of all of its parts suppliers together to voice opinions, discuss problems, exchange ideas, and generally improve relations. Later, Toyota worked especially hard to develop supply contracts with local high-tech auto parts manufacturers.

These contracts enabled Toyota to add production facilities for engines and steering systems in 1987, which were slated to begin full-fledged production in 1991 with a local content ratio as high as 75 percent. In response to Toyota's difficulties in finding local auto parts companies to meet its needs, several of Toyota's main parts suppliers in Japan initiated plans to set up their own factories near Toyota's facilities in Kentucky. To avoid stirring up local resentment and trade friction, only three (Nippondenso, Toyoda Gosei, and Aisin Seiki) set up plants of their own, while other affiliated members set up facilities via joint-venture or technology-transfer deals with local auto parts companies.

How did Toyota deal with labor relations? First, Toyota chose to set up shop in Kentucky, a state with a very low UAW unionization rate. Next, Toyota built upon the relations it had developed with the UAW when establishing NUMMI. These two measures greatly reduced the number of labor relations problems to be dealt with. At NUMMI, Toyota had to accommodate GM's closed-shop union policy by agreeing to a hiring plan that made 800 of NUMMI's initial total of 1,200 employees former GM employees and that allowed 900 (75 percent) to be UAW members. This is why it took Toyota a full year of negotiations to get GM and the UAW to seriously consider introducing a Japanese-style production system.

Finally, an agreement was reached to depart from traditional union-oriented hiring practices and to adopt a Japanese-style labor agreement. This agreement reduced the number of job classifications to four. (Previously, GM had over thirty job classifications.) It also allowed the introduction of standard operations, multiple skills training, multiprocess handling, employee teams, and a suggestion system, while receiving a commitment from employees to avoid strikes. Toyota did not insist on a completely Japanese-style production system. For example, they agreed to do away with alternating day and night shifts and other practices that were seen as incompatible with U.S. lifestyles. Other compromises were negotiated and agreed upon.

How did Toyota approach the issues of personnel training? Toyota emphasizes demonstration and hands-on learning in its personnel training, and before starting production at the NUMMI plant Toyota hosted a "leaders class" in Japan for some 240 NUMMI employees. Toyota also worked out an agreement with the UAW that enabled training instructors to be sent to NUMMI from Japan. These instructors showed NUMMI employees the details of how the Toyota production system would work in their own plant.

Finally, Toyota took various measures to blend in harmoniously with the local community. Instead of following the

Japanese corporate tradition of sending employees from Japan to live near each other and without their families — a tradition that makes it too easy for Japanese employees to stick together as an insular expatriate group and does not encourage them to form friendships with local people — Toyota sent employees with their families and made sure they lived in places where their neighbors were Americans.

Toyota also established a hot line system by which local employees could make their suggestions and complaints heard. The hot line system itself is based on a suggestion made by a local employee. The system is composed of a network of hot line telephones, one at each factory or office, that employees can pick up anytime to voice suggestions or complaints. Messages are recorded on an answering machine and reviewed by the relevant managers. This system has been well received. Toyota also helps maintain good labor-management relations through traditional Japanese customs such as sending seasonal greeting cards to employees. In an American adaptation, the Christmas cards include turkey coupons.

Notes

Chapter 2

1. See Chapter 2 in Masaaki Imai's *Kaizen: The Key to Japan's Competitive Success* (New York: Random House Business Division, 1986). In the glossary he defines kaizen as continuing improvement in personal life, home life, social life, and working life. When applied to the workplace, kaizen means continuing improvement involving everyone — managers and workers alike. Further, he says, improvement can be defined as kaizen and innovation, where a kaizen strategy maintains and improves the working standard through small, gradual improvements, and innovation calls forth radical improvements as a result of large investments in technology.

2. See Yasuhiro Monden, *Applying Just-in-Time: The Japanese-American Experience* (Norcross, GA: Industrial Engineering and Management Press, 1986), p. 17. This is the first paper published in the United States to describe Japanese target costing and kaizen costing. (These terms literally were

translated from the Japanese terms "cost planning" and "cost improvement.")

In addition, see Y. Noboru and Y. Monden's chapter "Daihatsu Kogyo: Jidosha kigyo no genkakanri" (Daihatsu Motors: Cost management in an auto company) in Okamoto, Miyamoto, and Sakurai's text on high-tech accounting, *Haitekukaikei* (Tokyo: Doyuken, 1987). Some of this material is available in English in Yasuhiro Monden, *Applying Just-in-Time: The Japanese-American Experience* (Norcross, GA: Industrial Engineering and Management Press, 1986) and Y. Monden and M. Sakurai, eds., *Japanese Management Accounting: A World Class Approach to Profit Management* (Cambridge, MA: Productivity Press, 1989).

Also, in his article "Target Costing and How to Use It" (*Journal of Cost Management*, Summer 1989), Michiharu Sakurai covers target costing in many Japanese assembly-type industries and computer software companies.

3. See Takao Makido's chapter "Recent Trends in Japan's Cost Management Practices" in Monden and Sakurai, eds., *Japanese Management Accounting: A World Class Approach to Profit Management*, pp. 3-13.

4. See the following:

Monden and Sakurai, eds., *Japanese Management Accounting*, Chapter 2 ("Total Cost Management System in Japanese Automobile Corporations").

Yoshiteru Noboru and Y. Monden's chapter "Daihatsu Kogyo: Jidosha kigyo no genkakanri" (Daihatsu Motors: Cost management in an auto company), in Okamoto, Miyamoto, and Sakurai, *Haitekukaikei*.

5. For example, read about target development in Masayasu Tanaka's chapter "Cost Planning and Control Systems in the Design Phase of a New Product" in Monden and Sakurai, eds., *Japanese Management Accounting*.

6. Some companies distinguish VA from VE as described.
7. For example, see Takao Tanaka's "Toyota no kaizen yosan" (Toyota's kaizen budget), *Kigyokaikei*, Volume 42, Number 3, 1990.
8. For detail characteristics of Japanese-style MBO, see Y. Monden's chapter "Characteristics of Performance Control Systems in Japanese Corporations" in Monden and Sakurai, eds. *Japanese Management Accounting*, pp. 413-423.
9. Among Japanese automakers each process shown in Figure 2-7 constitutes the "process" in the process-costing system and each process is headed by a foreman.
10. Managers also have objectives of quality and productivity (efficiency or lead-time reduction) as well as a kaizen cost target.

Chapter 4

1. See the July 12, 1989 issue of *Seisansei Shimbun (Productivity newspaper)*, published by the Japan Productivity Center.
2. See the August 16, 1989 issue of *Seisansei Shimbun*.
3. See Kazuo Mizoguchi's *Nyumon rieki keikaku* (Introduction to profit planning). (Chuo Keizai-sha, 1980), pp. 202-205.
4. Mizoguchi, *Nyumon rieki keikaku*, pp. 208-215.
5. See Shoichi Terayama's article "Toyota jidosha: Genten jinji no daikigyo-byo o kokufuku dekiru ka?" ("Can Toyota overcome the large-company syndrome with its new streamlined personnel system?") in *Nikkei Business Magazine*, pp. 46-47.
6. See Note 1.
7. See the November 2, 1989 issue of *Nihon Keizai Shimbun* (also called Nikkei Shimbun or Japan Economic Newspaper).
8. See the November 11, 1989 issue of *Nihon Keizai Shimbun*.
9. See Note 8.

Chapter 7

1. See the following:

   Mitsuru Okano and Katsuo Yamamoto's "Kumitate-kako-kensa shisutemu no saishin gijutsu" (Latest technology for assembly/processing/inspection systems).

   Shigeru Watanabe and Yuzuru Akiyama, *Seisan shisutemu to saishin jidoka gijutsu* (Production systems and recent automation technologies), (1986), pp. 167- 190.

2. See Yoshinori Okada and Toshikazu Sasaki, "Matsuda in okeru seisan joho kanri no jissai" (Facts about production information management at Mazda), *Production Management* (Japan Management Association, July 1986), pp. 77-83.

3. See Kanto Information System Division, "Fukaura kojo ni okeru ALC shisutemu" (ALC system at the Fukaura plant), (Kanto Auto Works, November 1989).

4. See Eiichi Sumibe, "Sei-han ittaika o mezasu senryaku-teki joho shisutemu no tenkai" (Development of a strategic information system to integrate production and sales), *Nihon Keizai Shimbun*, September 24, 1990.

5. This material is excerpted from a presentation made by Hirotada Takahashi and Hiroyoshi Kubota, "ALC shisutemu ni tsuite" (About ALC systems), on December 12, 1990, at a seminar on the Toyota Production System held by the Tokyo Management Council.

6. This information comes from a paper by Yasuo Fukuoka, "Toyota jidosha KK ni okeru ALC shisutemu no kochiku" (Structure of the ALC system at Toyota), presented at the 1990 Fujitsu CIM Symposium in Osaka.

7. See Y. Monden, *Toyota Production System*. 2nd ed. (Norcross, GA: Industrial Engineering and Management Press, 1992).

Bibliography

Aono, Toyosaku. Toyota hanbai senryaku (Toyota sales strategy). Tokyo: Diamond-sha, 1982.

Ban, S., and Kimura, O. "Toyota jidosha seisanbumon: Kihon nokettei to jyunansei no torikumi" (Toyota manufacturing division: Learning the fundamentals and incorporation of flexibility). *JMA Production Management* (October 1986): 13-22.

Furukawa, Eichi, et al. "Kokusai seisan seiko e no shishin o saguru" (Looking for the road to success in international production). *IE Review* (Vol. 30, No. 5, December 1989).

Honjo, Jiro. Toyota no hanbairyoku-tsuyosa no himitsu (The secret of Toyota's sales strength). Tokyo: Nisshin Hodo, 1988.

Ikari, Yoshiaki. Kaihatsu Nanbaa 179 A: Karoora no michi (Development No. 179A: The road to a new Corolla).Tokyo: Bungei Shunju, 1983.

Ikari, Yoshiaki. Toyota tai Nissan: Shinsha kaihatsu no saizen sen (Toyota versus Nissan: The leadership race in new car development). Tokyo: Diamond-sha, 1985.

Imai, Masaaki. Kaizen: The Key to Japan's Competitive Success. New York: Random House Business Division, 1986.

Japan Management Association (eds.). *Ajia NICS ni okeru kigyo senryaku* (Corporate strategies among the Asian NICs). Tokyo: 1987.

―――. *Hokubei ni okeru kigyo senryaku* (Corporate strategies in North America). Tokyo: 1987.

Kaneko, Shozo. *Toyota vs. GM 21 seiki e no taiketsu* (Toyota versus GM: Showdown for the twenty-first century). Nippon Jitsugyo Shuppan-sha, 1986.

Kato, Y. "Genkakikaku-katsudo no shintenkai: Daihatsu kogyo no jirei" (New development of target costing activities: The case of Daihatsu). *Kaikei* (Vol. 138, No. 4, 1990): 46-62.

Kohno, Toyohiro. *Shin seihin kaihatsu senryaku* (New product development strategy). Tokyo: Diamond-sha, 1987.

Kusunoki, Kaneyoshi. "Kokusai jidai no seisan taio" (Production response to an international era). *IE Review* (Vol. 30, No. 5, December 1989).

Makido, Takao. "Recent Trends in Japan's Cost ManagemePractices." In Y. Monden and M. Sakurai, eds., *Japanese Management Accounting*. Cambridge: Productivity Press, 1989, 3-13.

Miles, Lawrence D. *Techniques of Value Analysis and Engineering*. New York: McGraw-Hill, 1961.

Monden, Yasuhiro. *Applying Just-In-Time: The American/Japanese Experience*. Norcross, GA: Industrial Engineering and Management Press, 1986.

―――. "Characteristics of Performance Control Systems in Japanese Corporations." In Y. Monden and M. Sakurai, eds., *Japanese Management Accounting*, Cambridge: Productivity Press, 1989, 413-423.

―――. "Cost Accounting and Control in the Just-in-Time Production System: The Daihatsu Kogyo Experience." In Y.

Monden and M. Sakurai, eds., *Japanese Management Accounting*, Cambridge: Productivity Press, 35-48.

———. *Cost Management in the New Manufacturing Age: Innovations in the Japanese Automobile Industry*. Cambridge: Productivity Press, 1992.

———. "Functional Management to Promote Company-Wide Quality Control and Cost Management," from *Toyota Production System*. Norcross, GA: Industrial Engineering and Management Press, 1993. Second edition.

———. "JIT seisan hoshiki to genkakeisan, genkakanri" (JIT production system, cost accounting, and cost management). *Kigyokaikei* (Vol. 40, No. 5, 1988): 24-32.

———. "Kanada ni okeru Nippon no jidosha meka to buhin meka no seisan senryaku" (Production strategies of Japanese automobile and auto parts manufacturers in Canada). *Kosei Torihiki* (Fair Trade). (No. 434, December 1986): 29-35.

———. "Seisan senryaku no kokusaika" (Internationaliz-ation of production strategies). *Corporate Management's International Strategies* by Shibakawa, Rinya, and Takayanagi, Akira. Tokyo: Dobunkan, 1987.

———. "Target Costing and Kaizen Costing in Japanese Automobile Companies," *Journal of Management Accounting Research*. (Vol. 3, Fall, 1991).

———. "Total Cost Management System in Japanese Automobile Corporations." In *Applying Just-In-Time* by Y. Monden, 171-184, and Y. Monden and M. Sakurai, eds., *Japanese Management Accounting*, Cambridge: Productivity Press, 1989, 15-33.

———. *Toyota Production System*. Norcross, GA: Industrial Engineering and Management Press, 1983.

Monden, Yasuhiro, and Sakurai, Michiharu, eds., *Japanese Management Accounting: A World Class Approach to Profit Management*. Cambridge: Productivity Press, 1989.

Morozumi, Takehiko. "Nyu moderu ga dekiru made: Serika keiretsu no baai" (The development story of the new line of Toyota Celica cars). *Motoru Fuan* (Motor Fan) (Vol. 33, No. 1, January 1990).

Nakata, Yoshinori, and Monden, Yasuhiro. "Jidosha kigyo no maaketeingu senryaku: Toyota no jirei no ronriteki bunseki" (Marketing strategy at an automobile company: Analysis of Toyota case studies). *Keiei Kodo* (Managerial Behavior) (Vol. 4, No. 3, 1989): 21-30.

Nissan Motor Co., Ltd. *Annual Securities Report: March 1990.* Ministry of Finance Printing Office, July 1991.

Noboru, Yoshiteru, and Monden, Yasuhiro. "Jidosha kogyo ni okeru sogoteki genkakanri system" (Total cost management system in Japanese automobile corporations) *Kigyokaikei* (Vol. 35, No. 2, 1983): 104-112.

———. "Daihatsu Kogyo: Jidosha kigyo no genkakanri" (Daihatsu Motors: Cost management in an auto company). In *Haitekukaikei.* Okamoto, Miyamoto, and Sakurai, eds., Tokyo: Doyuken, 1987, 272-289.

Noguchi, Noboru. *Jidosha gyokai wa wndaka, shijo howa o do norikiru ka* (How will the Japanese auto industry survive yen appreciation and market saturation?). Tokyo: Nippon Jitsugyo Shuppan-sha, 1986.

Okamoto, M., Miyamoto, M., and Sakurai, M., eds., *Haitekukaikei* (High-Tech Accounting). Tokyo: Doyukan, 1987.

Roos, Daniel; Womack, James P.; and Jones, Daniel T. *The Machine that Changed the World.* New York: Macmillan, 1990.

Sakurai, Michiharu. "Target Costing and How to Use It." *Journal of Cost Management* (Summer 1989): 39-50.

Shibata, Koichiro; Omichi, Yasunori; and Ishiro, Masaharu. *Jidosha* (Automobiles). Tokyo: Nippon Keizai Shimbunsha, 1986.

Shiozawa, Shigeru. *Toyota Jidosha kaihatsu shusa seido* (Toyota Motor's development chief system). Tokyo: Kodansha, 1987.

Takeuchi, Toshio. *Jidosha hanbai* (Automobile sales). Tokyo: Nihon Keizai Shimbun-sha, 1986.

Tanaka, Masayasu. "Nihon kigyo no shinseihin-kaihatu ni okeru Genkakanri" (Cost management in the new product development of Japanese companies). *Kigyokaikei* (Vol. 41, No. 2, 1989): 19-25.

―――. "Cost planning and control systems in the design-phase of a new product." In *Japanese Management Accounting*, Cambridge: Producitivity Press, 49-71.

Tanaka, Takao. "Toyota no kaizen yosan" (Kaizen budget of Toyota). *Kigyokaikei* (Vol. 42, No. 3, 1990a): 59-66.

―――. "Jidosha-maker ni okeru shinseihin kaihatsu to mokuhyo-genka: Toyota no kenkakikaku" (New product development and target costs in an auto company: Target costing at Toyota). *Kigyokaikei* (Vol. 42, No. 10, 1990b): 46-62.

Toyota Motor Corporation, ed. *Annual Securities Report* (June 1982 to June 1988). Tokyo: Ministry of Finance Printing Office.

―――. *Annual Securities Report* (June 1990). Tokyo: Ministry of Finance Printing Office, 1991.

―――. *Sozo kagiri-naku: Toyota Jidosha 30 nen shi* (Unlimited creativity: A thirty-year history of Toyota). Toyota City: Toyota Motors, 1967.

―――. *Sozo kagiri-naku: Toyota Jidosha 50 nen shi* (Unlimited creativity: A fifty-year history of Toyota). Toyota City: Toyota Motors, 1987.

About the Author

Yasuhiro Monden is professor of managerial accounting and production management at the University of Tsukuba's Institute of Socio-Economic Planning. He received his doctorate from the University of Tsukuba, where he also served as dean of the Graduate Program of Management Sciences and Public Policy Studies.

Dr. Monden has gained valuable practical knowledge and experience from his research and related activities in the Japanese automobile industry. He was instrumental in introducing the just-in-time (JIT) production system to the United States. His English-language book *Toyota Production System* is recognized as a JIT classic and was awarded the 1984 Nikkei Prize by the *Nikkei Economic Journal*. Recent books include *Japanese Management Accounting: A World Class Approach to Profit Management* (1989) and *Cost Management in the New Manufacturing Age: Innovations in the Japanese Automobile Industry* (1992), published by Productivity Press.

Dr. Monden taught at California State University at Los Angeles in 1991 and 1992. Previously he was a visiting professor at the State University of New York at Buffalo in 1980 and

1981. He is an adviser for the Production and Operations Management Society (POMS) and has been an international director of the management accounting section of the American Accounting Association. He serves on the editorial board of the AAA's *Journal of Management Accounting Research*.

Professor Yasuhiro Monden, Institute of Socio-Economic Planning, University of Tsukuba, Tsukuba-shi, Ibaraki 305, Japan.

Index

Printed in the United States
50862LVS00006B/37-84

9 781563 271397